IMPROVING STUDENTS' WEB USE AND INFORMATION LITERACY

IMPROVING STUDENTS' WEB USE AND INFORMATION LITERACY

A GUIDE FOR TEACHERS AND TEACHER LIBRARIANS

JAMES E. HERRING

facet publishing

© James Herring 2011
Published by Facet Publishing
7 Ridgmount Street, London WC1E 7AE
www.facetpublishing.co.uk

Facet Publishing is wholly owned by CILIP: the Chartered Institute of Library and Information Professionals.

British Library Cataloguing in Publication Data
A catalogue record for this book is available from the British Library.

ISBN 978-1-85604-743-2

First published 2011
Reprinted digitally thereafter

Text printed on FSC accredited material.

Mixed Sources
Product group from well-managed forests and other controlled sources
www.fsc.org Cert no. SA-COC-1565
© 1996 Forest Stewardship Council
FSC

Typeset from author's files in 10/14 pt Constantia and Myriad Pro
by Facet Publishing Production.
Printed and made in Great Britain by MPG Books Group, UK.

This book is dedicated to my wife, Val
Writing a book is much easier than running a marathon

Contents

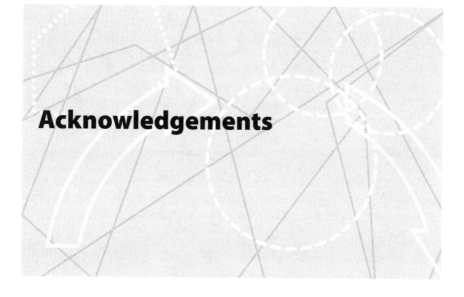

Acknowledgements

I would like to thank all the people who supplied me with material for this book. I have not been able to use everything sent to me because of space restrictions. In particular, I would like to thank the following people for their advice and examples which they so generously provided: Anne-Marie Tarter, Stephanie Bush, Anne Robinson, Carolyn Farrugia, Raylene Neville, Margaret Lincoln, Marie Slim, Lee Fitzgerald, Carol Kuhlthau, Ian McLean, Sarah Elliott, Paul Potaka, Randi Schmidt, Ginny Kowlalski, Andrew Dutcher, Kathy Schrock, Ryan Flood, Colleen Foley, Tom Driscoll, Peter Pappas, Bente Pederson, Cheri Horyna, Jane Coyle and Julie Ferrone.

As ever, Helen Carley, Lin Franklin and Kathryn Beecroft at Facet Publishing have provided great help.

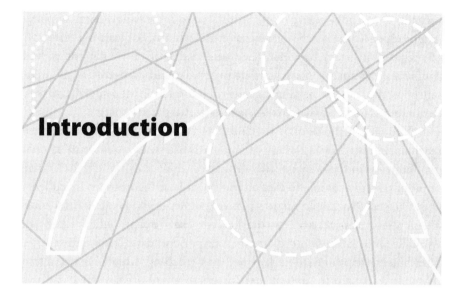

Introduction

The aims of this book

The growth of the internet and particularly the web, and the increasing need for students and staff in schools to be able to use information effectively when they study, work or socialize, has meant that there is now a greater recognition of the need for information literacy and web use to be seen as key aspects of modern education and society. Most studies of the ability and competency of teachers and teacher librarians (including school librarians and school library media specialists) to use the web effectively show that school staff need advice, guidance and in-service training. Similarly, most research on students' use of information literacy skills, including effective web use, demonstrates that most students do not use the web effectively, and are unlikely to transfer what they are taught about web use across the subjects which they are studying. The primary aim of this book is to provide schools with a practical guide, built on a sound theoretical base, to developing better use of the web by staff and students, in order to improve learning and teaching in schools. The aim is to change staff and students in schools from web *users* to critical web *learners*.

This book also aims to raise the profile of information literacy in schools, with a view to persuading teachers, teacher librarians and school management that information literacy skills and abilities should be a key focus in the school curriculum. Students are increasingly seen as being independent learners, who make use of the vast array of learning resources of the web, in order to widen their knowledge of curricular topics and complete assignments. If students are to be web-alert, web-critical and web-reflective, they need to be taught a range of information literacy skills, so they can develop abilities which make them reflective practitioners.

A third aim of the book is twofold. First, it is intended to provide new teachers and teacher librarians (including those studying for professional qualifications in these areas) with a resource which they can use for a range of purposes, for example to expand their own learning or to teach students about web use. The book contains many examples of good practice in schools and new teachers and teacher librarians can use or adapt them in their own work. Second, it aims to provide more experienced teachers and teacher librarians with an update on learning and teaching, which can serve as a refresher and help to update their practice. There are several ideas and examples which they can use to extend their knowledge of information literacy and use of the web, and their ability to use Web 2.0 tools. All teachers and teacher librarians will be able to use the book's ideas, examples and approaches to improve the ways in which their students learn about using the web.

The structure of the book

The first part of the book is aimed at developing the knowledge, skills and abilities of teachers and teacher librarians. Chapter 1 provides a context for the book – learning and teaching in schools – to which the rest of the book relates, and allows teachers and teacher librarians to focus on the fundamental issues of today's schooling, of which web use is one. Chapter 2 seeks to develop teachers and teacher librarians (and other school staff) as effective web users, in particular effective web searchers. If school staff lack expertise in web use, they are unlikely to be able to improve their students' use of the web. Chapter 3 focuses on website evaluation, which is increasingly important for teachers and teacher librarians given the continued explosion in the availability of *potentially* useful material on the web. Chapter 4 examines the diverse nature of Web 2.0 and how schools might exploit this new development, and gives international examples of the use of Web 2.0 tools. Chapter 5 examines the theory and practice of information literacy in schools. It provides teachers and teacher librarians with new knowledge of aspects of information literacy, and gives examples for them to adopt or adapt for their own schools.

The second part of the book focuses on developing students as reflective users of information literacy skills and abilities, including making reflective use of the web. Chapter 6 looks at the challenges faced in improving students as web users and the examples can be used in a practical manner by teachers and teacher librarians. Chapter 7 seeks to explore the development of learning websites by teachers and teacher librarians, and emphasises the importance of developing learning resources to meet the needs of particular groups of students in schools. This chapter examines the use of a range of tools and packages, which teachers and teacher librarians can use collaboratively. In Chapter 8 the focus is on the content of learning websites, in particular extending the use of pathfinders, by integrating them into learning websites, which serve a range of student needs, and connect learning resources much more to the subjects being studied in schools. Finally, Chapter 9 looks forward to the next phase of information and communication technologies (ICT) in schools, examining future web development and the future roles of teachers and teacher librarians.

Who should read this book?

Although the main audience for this book will be teachers and teacher librarians in countries across the world, who will benefit from the many international examples provided, school managers will also benefit from reading it so they have an overview of the importance of information literacy and ensure that it is adequately taught in the school curriculum. The book will also be of use to school ICT managers who can use the ideas and practical guidance to train school staff in using Web 2.0 tools in particular. It should be viewed as a key resource in schools, with multiple uses, as it emphasizes throughout how teachers and teacher librarians can learn together and collaboratively develop learning resources for students in schools. The book should be on reading lists for courses on teacher education, teacher librarianship and how to develop ICT in schools, so students can use its ideas and examples to give them a sound basis for future practice.

The big picture: learning and teaching in today's schools

Having read this chapter you will be able to:

- refresh your views on the purposes of education
- reflect on current theories of learning in schools
- link your knowledge of learning with web use and information literacy skills
- examine a range of current views on teaching in schools
- identify where you can incorporate ICT into your teaching
- reflect on collaboration between teachers and teacher librarians.

Introduction

Teachers and teacher librarians in schools across the world are faced with an ever increasing number of initiatives from local and central governments. They are also encouraged to link these initiatives to greater use of ICT in the school. Therefore teachers and teacher librarians are often so busy keeping up with current trends and new technological initiatives that they are in danger of losing sight of the key purposes of education and the key aims of their school. The use of ICT in schools is now often viewed as a *sine qua non* for learning and teaching. Staff are reminded of the cost of ICT developments and it may appear that teachers and teacher librarians must use ICT developments such as interactive whiteboards because they are expensive and therefore that expense must be justified. There is also pressure on teachers and teacher librarians to be seen to be using ICT in their teaching, but this use of ICT can often be superficial, for example when they use an interactive whiteboard merely to replicate what was previously done with a laptop and a projector. Thus the way in which ICT can be used to meet the school's aims and promote better learning and teaching in the school should be emphasized.

In most schools teaching students how to use the web has moved on from isolated classes in a computer lab where students were taught the technical aspects of using Google, how to bookmark sites, and how to cut and paste information. One of the problems schools often face, however, is that although students now use the web for all mainstream subjects, there is often no systematic approach to teaching web use. Teacher librarians in schools may attempt to teach information literacy skills, including web use, but there are only sporadic instances of teachers either developing or reinforcing these skills.

Web use and information literacy skills should be part of each student's learning and the focus in schools should be on how students can use information literacy skills to enhance their learning. Learning from e-resources is the key educational factor here, not the student's increased use of the web. Teachers and teacher librarians who reflect on how effectively their students learn, and not just on what the students learn, and who also reflect on their own teaching, will be making a greater contribution to the overall aim of the school: to educate students.

This chapter will briefly outline the purposes of schools in the 21st century; review current theories of learning, learning styles and ICT and learning; and examine theories of and approaches to teaching in schools, including styles of teaching and using ICT in teaching.

The purposes of education and schools

In most countries there is an acceptance that the education of children is a valued aspect of society. Formal education is carried out in schools and informal education takes place in society as a whole. Examining the purposes of education and schools can provide teachers and teacher librarians with a big picture view of their roles in schools and can provide a context for what they do in schools. Ryan and Cooper argue that there is a wide range of views on the purposes of education, and define education as 'a process of human growth by which one gains greater understanding and control over oneself and one's world' (2010, 31). They compare education with schooling and argue that education is something which happens before and after people attend school. The purposes of education may be seen as encouraging people to relate well to others, to understand their society and to engage in formal or informal lifelong learning.

The purposes of schools can be seen as being narrower than the purposes of education, for three reasons. First, schools deal with students over a particular period of time, whereas education takes place during a person's whole life. Second, schools engage students when they are young – usually around age 5 to 18 – and still developing physically and intellectually. Third, education is compulsory in all countries, although economics dictate that some children may be prevented from attending school in some societies. Post school education is voluntary and informal education takes place over a lifetime for most people.

What then are the key purposes of schools? Ryan and Cooper identify four:

- ◆ 'intellectual purposes' – producing students who can undertake academically challenging work
- ◆ 'political and civic purposes' – producing students who will take an interest in society when they leave school and be active citizens
- ◆ 'economic purposes' – developing students as the future workforce in their society and who will increase society's overall wealth
- ◆ 'social purposes' – teaching students to develop socially acceptable habits, such as respect for others' opinions, good behaviour, cooperation such as sharing ideas, and concern for others' wellbeing (2010, 38–42).

Spence speaks of 'the physical, social, emotional, academic and cultural needs of our students' (2009, 55). In the context of teachers and teacher librarians developing students who are effective users of information literacy skills, it is clear that teaching these skills can improve students' academic work, extend their knowledge of active citizenship, prepare them for the workplace, where effective information practices are increasingly important, and encourage good social habits in areas such as sharing websites or social networking etiquette. Identifying how information literacy skills, including web use, fit into the overall purposes of the school can enable teachers and teacher librarians to meet wider aims, for example encouraging students to apply their information literacy skills to all subjects, and from school to work.

Learning theories

There is a vast literature on learning in schools and many definitions of learning. Pritchard includes the following as good examples of the definitions of learning:

◆ a change in behaviour as a result of experience or practice
◆ knowledge gained through study
◆ gaining knowledge of, or skill in, something through study, teaching, instruction or experience
◆ the individual process of constructing understanding based on experience from a wide range of sources (2009, 2).

There is no one agreed definition of learning and it is important to recognize that learning is a complex concept and practice. However, thinking about what learning might be and how it might be best encouraged in the classroom or school library is important for teachers and teacher librarians, as developing students as effective learners is a key purpose of school education.

Behaviourism

Learning theories can be broadly grouped into behaviourism and constructivism. James states that behaviourism is 'mostly concerned with behaviour, not what goes on in a person's head' (2007, 17), and that behaviourism focuses on providing rewards to students, separating parts of complex ideas and skills into small sections, and that students should be asked to focus on basic skills, often through rote learning. Behaviourism views students as receivers of knowledge from the teacher and it views knowledge – what students can learn – as being something which is accessed externally by students, and not constructed by them. This approach to learning is based on stimuli, which can be positive (rewarding students for learning well) or negative (withholding rewards from or punishing students who do not learn well).

Examples of behavioural approaches in schools are when students are told to learn arithmetical tables or remember formulae by rote. Examples of behavioural approaches being used when teaching information literacy skills are students being asked to try to remember Dewey classification numbers or to write down explanations of an information literacy model. The intention is to help students but it is unlikely that students will be motivated to learn in this way. The same applies to web use by students. Although students may learn how to use the web in a mechanical way through behaviourist approaches (for example being given a list of rules to follow when accessing websites), students are not likely to become effective web users when taught in this way. In general, behavioural approaches in education are now seen as outdated.

Constructivism

Although there are many forms of constructivism in learning theories, social constructivism takes the view that learners are not merely receptacles of knowledge passed on by a teacher, but are conscious constructors of knowledge. This is a major difference between behaviourism and constructivism. Pritchard argues that 'In the context of constructivist theory, learning is an active, not a passive activity' (2009, 29). The key aspects of constructivist learning are that:

- prior learning is a key factor as students construct new knowledge from what they know already
- students will (if encouraged) make connections between areas of knowledge and reflect on them
- the social context of students' learning is important in influencing how students learn

◆ learning is very personal and students who are effective learners will be able to reflect on their own learning.

If we are to encourage our students to be reflective users of information literacy skills, including using the web, then it is important that teachers and teacher librarians take a social constructivist approach to learning. If we view students as constructing their own knowledge and building on prior knowledge, then this will have an influence on how students will be encouraged to use information literacy skills. Thus getting students to reflect on an information literacy skills model, such as this author's PLUS (Purpose, Location, Use and Self-evaluation) model (Herring, 2004), can encourage students to think about what their own individual model of learning might be.

Learning theories, in the context of the development of information literacy skills in schools, should not be seen as abstract concepts, but as the basis on which teachers and teacher librarians design and develop opportunities for students to learn to be effective learners.

Teaching in schools

One of the key ways in which the purposes of schools, as discussed above, can be met is through quality teaching in schools. Just as students need to be effective learners, teachers and teacher librarians need to be effective teachers. This applies not only to parts of the world such as North America and Australia, where most schools have teacher librarians who are qualified teachers, but also in areas such as the UK and New Zealand, where school librarians do not normally have a teaching qualification. This section seeks to refresh the thinking of teachers, teacher librarians and school librarians on the key aspects of teaching, particularly in relation to teaching information literacy.

What makes a good teacher?

Capel and Leask (2005) state that there are fundamental aspects of teaching which apply to all teachers, but also that different teachers often have individual approaches. The question might be asked – what makes a good teacher? They argue that a good teacher is one whose 'job is first and foremost to ensure that pupils learn' (2005, 8). These authors state that good teachers effectively carry out a range of duties including:

- subject teaching
- lesson preparation
- setting and marking of homework
- assessing pupil progress in a variety of ways
- writing reports
- recording achievement
- working as part of a subject team
- curriculum development and planning
- keeping up to date (often through work with the subject association)
- implementing school policies
- extracurricular activities (13).

There is no one definition of a good teacher, but in general good teachers are knowledgeable about their subject, interested in it, collaborative members of staff, well organized, and adaptable to new school policies and new technology, and have a sound understanding of students' needs.

What do teachers do?

Killen identifies a number of steps that effective teachers take in order to focus their teaching on student learning, and states that the first step is 'to describe what it is you want your students to understand' (2007, 13). This is more difficult than it might appear as the teacher or teacher librarian needs to be able to express themselves in a way that all students will understand. For example, if a teacher or teacher librarian is attempting to get students to understand the importance of planning an assignment, then they will explain this more than once, first in general terms that most students except possibly the less able ones will understand, then second in more specific terms so that the less able students will also understand. Effective teachers and teacher librarians will also check that students understand what they have said by asking questions.

Killen's second step is 'selecting content (or teaching topics) that will be a suitable vehicle for helping students gain the understanding that is described in your learning outcomes' (2007, 14). According to Killen the content selected by the teacher or teacher librarian should be of direct interest to students, and of a nature that can be explored through questions and studied in different ways, perhaps by students carrying out a range of activities. It should provide students with the opportunity to link with prior knowledge and relate to other areas of learning. Thus teaching students about assignment planning might involve gaining students' interest in the assignment, posing questions to them about what assignment planning is, and asking them to work in groups to brainstorm the subject and then write down their previous experience of doing assignments.

The third step Killen identified is to develop a suitable learning environment in which students will feel engaged in learning. This involves creating an atmosphere in which students will willingly reflect on their prior learning and discuss a range of aspects of the topic. In group work for assignment planning, for example, the teacher or teacher librarian might ask each group to draw up a concept map of assignment planning and use it to advise the other groups of what effective assignment planning might be. The fourth step is 'to give students opportunities to publicly demonstrate their developing understanding' (Killen, 15). This enables students to apply what they have learned, for example by drawing an individual concept map of a selected topic, and the teacher or teacher librarian to judge the students' levels of understanding, and take action where necessary.

Lesson planning is an important aspect of what teachers do as effective lesson planning is a prerequisite to successful teaching in the classroom or in the library. Butt (2006) outlines the key aspects of lesson planning as identifying the learning objectives of the lesson, planning the lesson effectively, choosing an appropriate approach, choosing appropriate techniques, and creating a suitable learning environment. He also provides examples of lesson plan templates. At its simplest this would be a list giving the time of the lesson, the group being taught, the aims and objectives of the lesson, the resources needed to teach it, the activities to be undertaken, and evaluation methods. Figure 1.1 shows a template for a more detailed lesson plan.

The key difference between the simple lesson plan and the more complex plan shown in Figure 1.1 is that the second plan provides scope for identifying much more detailed planning and reflection on the part of the teacher or teacher librarian taking the lesson.

Figure 1.2 shows an example of a lesson plan for a year 9 geography class, in which the teacher focuses on aspects of information literacy linked to the subject being taught. Incorporating information literacy skills into the curriculum is a very effective and meaningful way of introducing students to these skills.

Date	Lesson	Time	Class	Room
Title of lesson				
Lesson's aims				
Learning objectives and enquiry questions				

Subject content: National Curriculum/syllabus links	Cross curricular links/themes/competencies
Resources	Advanced preparation (room and equipment)
Differentiation	Action points

Learning activities/tasks	Time	Teaching strategies/actions

Assessment opportunities, objectives and evidence

Evaluation of learning	Evaluation of teaching

Action points

Figure 1.1 Lesson plan template (Butt, 2006, 29)

Incorporating the web into teaching

Teachers and teacher librarians can use the web in their teaching for a range of purposes. First, the web is a source of resources for personal staff development so teachers can extend their subject knowledge by finding websites or articles on the web. For example, an Australian geography teacher might use the Aussie Educator site (www.aussieeducator.org.au) to update her knowledge about volcanoes. In the UK, a geography teacher might use

Year 9 Geography –Information Literacy Activity

Title	Investigating Australia's Physical Environments - Natural Hazards (Floods) – Lesson 1 of 2		
Overview	This is the first in a series of two lesson's incorporating an information literacy activity. The focus is on Investigating Australia's Physical Environments', in particular Natural Hazards. In this lesson, students will gain an understanding of what conditions are needed to cause a flood.		
Topic	Investigating Australia's Physical Environments		
KLA	Human Society and its Environment	**Subject**	Geography
Year	9	**Stage**	5A1
Learning Outcomes	**5.1** Identifies, gathers and evaluates geographical information **5.2** Analyses, organises and synthesises geographical information **5.3** Selects and uses appropriate written, oral and graphic forms to communicate geographical information **5.4** Selects and applies appropriate geographical tools **5.6** Explains the geographical processes that form and transform Australian environments		
Students Learn About:	• the nature of the natural hazard in Australia • the geographical processes involved • the impacts of the natural hazard: – economic – environmental – social	**Students Learn To:**	• describe the geographical processes associated with the natural hazard • describe the economic, environmental and social impacts of the natural hazard in Australia
Duration	100 minutes		
Teacher Prep time	45 minutes		
Materials required	• Computers (Internet Access) • Maps • Photographs • Virtual Worksheet (Attachment 2)		
Procedure			

Figure 1.2 Example of a lesson plan for a year 9 geography class focusing on information literacy; this lesson plan is an example for student teachers at Southern Cross University Australia (www.scu.edu.au/library/download.php?doc_id=5553&site_id=40).

	1. A session must be pre-booked for a class space in a computer lab, or library computers
	2. Teacher sends an email (Attachment 1) to all students in the class at the beginning of the lesson, outlining instructions and providing links to WebPages.
	3. Attached to the email will be a "virtual worksheet" (Attachment 2) that students will complete and email back to the teacher before the start of next lesson.
	4. Teacher will assist students with any queries that arise throughout the lesson, and keep students on task by monitoring progress.
Homework:	• Students asked to complete the virtual worksheet as homework, if not done by the end of class
Suggested assessment::	
Attachments	• Virtual Worksheet • Instruction Email
Evaluation	
Author	ML
Creation Date	06/05/09

Figure 1.2 *(Continued)*

the Intute site (www.intute.ac.uk/) to increase her knowledge of population statistics, while a colleague in north America might use the extensive US Geological Survey site (http://education.usgs.gov) to find topical information on climate change. Similarly, teacher librarians may use the Resources for School Librarians site (www.sldirectory.com) for examples of information literacy teaching.

Second, the web can be a resource for teachers to plan activities for students in the classroom. They can avoid reinventing the wheel by searching for sites that will engage their students in meaningful activities. Wetzel focused on science teaching and the web and stated that students 'can explore science topics . . . in greater depth and more interactive ways – with, for instance, simulations, online projects and problem solving' (2005, 2). An example of activities provided by Wetzel is the Aerospace Lesson Plans site (http://quest.nasa.gov/aero/teachers/learning.html), where activities for all grades of students can be found and used by science teachers.

Third, the web can be used as a resource which provides students with mediated sites, which have been vetted by the teacher and, in many cases, the teacher librarian in a particular school. The value of this kind of mediation is that sites are selected for particular local purposes and to suit the learning needs of particular groups of students. As will be seen in Chapter 3, this kind of selection depends on teachers and teacher librarians being effective searchers of the web. For example, secondary or high school teachers seeking information for students on the abolition of slavery will increase the effectiveness of their search by including the term 'high school' in their search strategy, as this will produce results that include material specifically for high school students.

Wetzel (2005, 3) argues that using the web in science teaching benefits students and 'web based technology opens doors' by:

- providing equal access to information
- encouraging students to be active learners
- boosting students' motivation to learn
- supporting teachers' efforts to practise inquiry-based teaching and learning.

The first point is very important in schools across the world as, even in the so called 'developed' countries, many school students only have access to the web in school. Thus by providing equal access to all students, teachers and teacher librarians ensure a level playing field within the school. Active learning by students, with effective facilitation by teachers and teacher librarians, for example on the evaluation of web resources, has been shown to encourage students to learn more effectively. Students can be motivated by using web resources, but this will not happen automatically. Teacher librarians in particular will know that students who are left to search aimlessly in the library are likely to be less motivated to learn. However, if the use of the web is built into well structured lessons, which encourage students to question what they read and relate what they find on the web to prior learning in the classroom, then motivation is likely to be high.

Effective teachers and teacher librarians set appropriate challenges for students using the web, according to the abilities and learning styles of students. Wetzel (2004) claims that inquiry based teaching is the key to successful science education and this author would argue that it is one of the key elements in all school subjects. To be successful practitioners of inquiry based teaching, teachers and teacher librarians need to collaborate to ensure that their students have the requisite information literacy skills, abilities and techniques to use web resources effectively. Chapter 6 focuses on methods of teaching students these skills.

Collaboration between teachers and teacher librarians

One of the keys to successful teaching, particularly in relation to information literacy and students' use of the web, is for teachers and teacher librarians to collaborate. Montiel-Overall (2008) and Gibson-Langford (2007) identify a range of areas where teachers and teacher librarians can cooperate and collaborate. Both authors argue that cooperation between teachers and teacher librarians, for example where teacher librarians provides resources for the classroom, is much less effective than collaboration. Collaboration implies a sharing of knowledge between two professionals, for example the teacher's subject knowledge and the teacher librarian's knowledge of information literacy. When knowledge is shared, lessons or programmes can be jointly planned, with mutual understanding and a common terminology. It is very important to have a common terminology when teaching information literacy and web use to students. Thus, when teacher librarians introduce students to aspects of information literacy such as concept mapping or search strategy formulation, students are more likely to implement the skills they have been taught if teachers reinforce them in the classroom by using the same terms as those used by the teacher librarian. Examples of this type of collaboration will be given in Chapters 6–9.

Conclusion

Learning and teaching is the main basis for activities in schools and developing information literate students to be effective web users depends on schools having a clear focus on what students learn, how they learn, and what teaching strategies will be most effective. The challenge for teachers and teacher librarians is to create learning environments in the classroom and school library where students have access to relevant resources and learning scaffolds. This will enable students to use their information literacy skills and make effective use of the web in order to increase their learning.

References

Butt, G. (2006) *Lesson Planning*, 2nd edn, Continuum International.

Capel, S., Leask, M. and Turner, T. (1996) *Learning to Teach in the Secondary School: a companion to school experience*, Routledge.

Gibson-Langford, L. (2007) Collaboration: force or forced? Part 2, *Scan*, **27** (1), 31–7.

Herring, J. (2004) *The Internet and Information Skills: a guide for teachers and school librarians*, Facet Publishing.

James, M. (2007) *Improving Learning How to Learn: classrooms, schools and networks*, Routledge.

Killen, R. (2007) *Effective Teaching Strategies: lessons from research and practice*, 4th edn, Thomson Social Science Press.

Montiel-Overall, P. (2008) A Qualitative Study of Teacher and Librarian Collaboration, *Scan*, **27** (3), 25–31.

Pritchard, A. (2009) *Ways of Learning: learning theories and learning styles in the classroom*, 2nd edn, Routledge.

Ryan, K. and Cooper, J. (2010) *Those Who Can, Teach*, Wadsworth Cengage Learning.

Spence, C. (2009) *Leading with Passion and Purpose*, Pembroke Publishers.

Wetzel, D. (2005) *How to Weave the Web into K-8 Science*, vol. 2004, NSTA Press.

Finding and using information on the web

Having read this chapter you will be able to:

- be a more effective searcher for information on the web
- use search engines more effectively in your work as a teacher or teacher librarian
- use a greater range of sources for your teaching or when providing information to students
- understand how being a more effective searcher can help you exploit the web as a learning and teaching resource
- organize in-service sessions on web searching for staff in your school.

Introduction

The use of the web in today's schools by staff and students is now taken for granted and there is an assumption that all staff and students will be effective users of the web. Anecdotal evidence tends to suggest otherwise, however, and this author found when visiting several schools in different countries that many teachers and teacher librarians have limited abilities in searching effectively for information on the web. Staff in schools across the world often have very limited access to staff training that focuses on searching for information. Most staff are self-taught or have learned how to use search engines from colleagues whose experience may also be limited. It can be argued that there is a large opportunity cost for schools whose staff are not fully aware and fully equipped searchers of information on the web. Because there is so much free information on the web that can contribute to learning and teaching in schools, lack of expertise in searching can lead to many schools in effect losing out on finding out about concepts, ideas and experiences that could help staff improve their teaching and self development.

This chapter will seek to address the issues discussed above and provide a guide for increasing teachers' and teacher librarians' knowledge of search engines and directories, and improving their skills in searching for information on the web. It will also present an example of an in-service session on finding information on the web.

Search engines

The most common way to search for information in schools and society at large is by using a search engine, and by far the most popular search engine is Google. Notess defined a search engine as 'an Internet-based search box that provides text-match searching of its own crawler-built database of text-indexed Web pages [which provides access to] millions of freely accessible web pages' (2006, 98). An important point to be remembered in Notess' definition is that search engines provide text matching, which is different from keyword matching, and this is one reason why people are often disappointed by the ability of search engines to find relevant information about the keywords they have used. There is a vast range of search engines available on the web. For example The Search Engine List (www.thesearchenginelist.com) provides a list of over 100 search engines, and breaks them down into categories such as all purpose, books, business, enterprise, human search and metasearch engines. This site is useful as it reinforces an important point: although Google may be the most popular search engine in the world, it is not necessarily always the best search engine to use, particularly if the user is searching for specialist (for example medical) information. Figure 2.1 shows the specialist medical search engines in The Search Engine List. Although much of the information found in these search engines may also be found using Google, some information will not be found by Google. Senior students working on assignments related to particular aspects of medicine could well benefit from advice on how to use specialist search engines from the teacher librarian.

Bioinformatic Harvester	**Bioinformatic Harvester:** From the Karlsruhe Institute of Technology, the Bioinformatic Harvester crawls and crosslinks dozens of bioinformatic sites and serves 10's of thousands of pages daily.
Entrez	**Entrez (Pubmed):** The life sciences search engine.
EMBL-EBI	**EB-Eye** - EMBL-EBI's (European Bioinformatics Institute): Open-source, high-performance, full-featured text search engine library written entirely in Java. Very fast access to the EBI's data resources.
Genie Knows	**Genie Knows:** A division of IT Interactive Services Inc., a Canadian vertical search engine company concentrating on niche markets: health search, video games search, and local business directory search.
gɔpubmed	**GoPubMed:** Knowledge-based: GO - GeneOntology - Searching sorted - Social network and folsonomy for sciences.
healia	**Healia:** The health search engine. From the site, "The high quality and personalized health search engine".
KMLE Medical Dictionary King's Medical Library Engine	**KMLE (King's Medical Library Engine):** Full American Heritage Stedman's Medical Dictionary comprehensive resource including tens of thousands of audio pronunciations and abbreviation guides.
MeshPubMed	**MeSH** - Medical Subject Headings (GoPubMed): Knowledge-based.
Search Medica	**SearchMedica:** Professional Medical Search
WebMD	**WebMD:** A source for health information, a symptom checklist, pharmacy information, and a place to store personal medical information.The leading US Health portal, it scores over 40 million hits per month.

Figure 2.1 Medical search engines from The Search Engine List
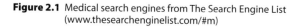
(www.thesearchenginelist.com/#m)

Google features
Google Advanced Search

Persuading teachers, teacher librarians and students *not* always to use Google can be a difficult task and one of the reasons for this is the array of very useful features offered by Google. This author argues that if school staff and students cannot be persuaded to use an alternative search engine (for example Dogpile at www.dogpile.com), then at least they should be persuaded not always to use Google's basic search facility. Google's advanced search feature has a number of advantages for searchers, one of which is that it slows those who use it down and immediately poses a challenge to them by asking them to consider their search in more detail. Do they want to search for:

◆ all these words
◆ this exact wording or phrase
◆ one or more of these words (see Figure 2.2)?

Thus Google, in presenting alternatives for the user – options which are not presented in the basic search facility – makes that user think more about the content of the search. The advantages of Google's advanced search feature for search strategies will be discussed below.

Google Advanced Search has three key features that are not available in the basic search: 'Language', 'File type' and 'Search within a site or domain'. The language tool can be used in schools for a variety of purposes. To use this option, the user clicks on the down arrow next to 'Language' (see Figure 2.2) and is

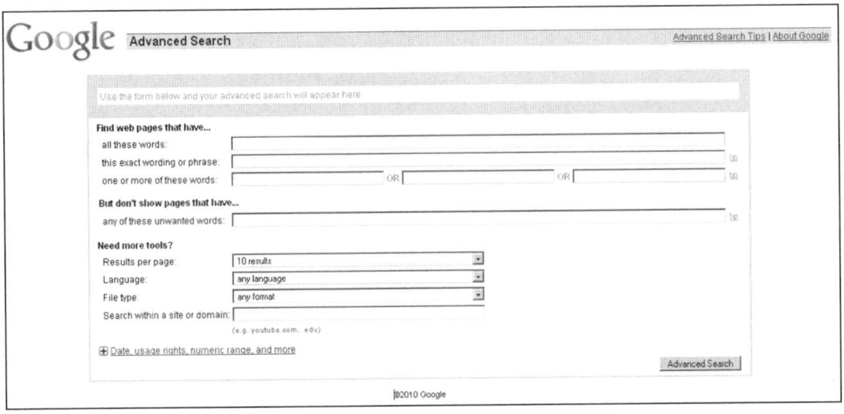

Figure 2.2 Google Advanced Search

presented with a vast array of languages. In this author's experience, very few modern language teachers know about this facility and very few teacher librarians use it. One way of using it would be to search for 'vacances en France' in the 'this exact wording or phrase' box, and use the language tool to specify that you want only to see results in French. Then the search will only present you with French websites. These sites could be used by language teachers as sources of fairly simple reading for students studying French. One could specify a language and then search for a newspaper from a particular country, town or city, or for an event, historical figure or geographical feature. After finding a range of sites on these topics, teachers and teacher librarians will be able to select levels of reading in the chosen language to suit a range of students. Once the language tool is no longer required, the user should click on the down arrow again and return to 'any language' (listed at the top), otherwise future searches will be carried out in the previously selected language.

The use of 'File type' is also underused in schools in this author's experience. When using this tool, which works in the same way as 'Language', the user is given a range of options, some of which might be useful; for example, Microsoft Powerpoint (sic) is on the list. The key value of this option is that staff in schools can search for material on curricular topics and find presentations given by staff in schools across the world. For example, a search for 'global warming high school' or 'global warming primary school' combined with file type Microsoft Powerpoint will find a list of presentations on the topic which have been presented in high schools or primary schools. Although there is no guarantee of quality in such presentations, most will be professionally put together and of potential use in the classroom as they are, or after being adapted for local use. It would be courteous to inform the author by email of any presentation that you use. After using this tool return to the 'any format' option.

The 'Search within a site or domain' tool can also be useful, particularly when searching very large sites such as government, university or major media sites in different countries. Table 2.1 lists some examples.

Thus a teacher or teacher librarian searching for federal government information on causes of drought in Australia would select the tool 'Search within a site or domain' and type in 'australia.gov.au' and then in the 'this exact wording or phrase' box type in 'causes of drought'. As can be seen from Figure 2.3, all the sites yielded from this search are from australia.gov.au. Thus if teachers or teachers librarians are seeking sites from a particular

Country	Government	University	Media
Australia	australia.gov.au (federal government) nsw.gov.au (state government, New South Wales)	csu.edu.au (Charles Sturt University) anu.edu.au (Australian National University)	abc.com.au (ABC TV and radio) smh.com.au (*Sydney Morning Herald* newspaper)
UK	direct.gov.uk (central government) scotland.gov.uk (regional government, Scotland)	ed.ac.uk (Edinburgh University) imperial.ac.uk (Imperial College London)	bbc.co.uk (BBC TV and radio) guardian.co.uk (*Guardian* newspaper)
USA	usa.gov (federal government) ca.gov (state government, California)	mit.edu (Massachusetts Institute of Technology) indiana.edu (Indiana University)	pbs.org (Public Broadcasting Service TV) nytimes.com (*New York Times* newspaper)

Table 2.1 Examples of government, university and media sites in Australia, the UK and the USA

perspective, such as central government, then searching using a site or domain can be very useful.

Examples seen in schools by this author include teachers encouraging students to examine a topic such as animal welfare by searching on the sites of a range of newspapers within their country or internationally; or teacher librarians creating e-pathfinders on curricular topics such as environmental protection, by searching through the sites of governments, newspapers and mining companies to gain a range of perspectives which students can study.

After using this facility, the user should clear the box with the site URL.

Google Images, Google Maps, Google Earth and Google News

Other features in Google which are often unexplored in schools include Google Images, and it is worth using Google Advanced Image Search, rather than the basic search, as it has many more options. Figure 2.4 shows the options available, which include searching by:

◆ content, such as news, photo content and clip art
◆ file type, such as.jpg
◆ domain, such as flickr.com or commons.wikimedia.org
◆ usage rights, such as images that are 'not filtered by license'.

Figure 2.3 Results of a domain search using Google Advanced Search

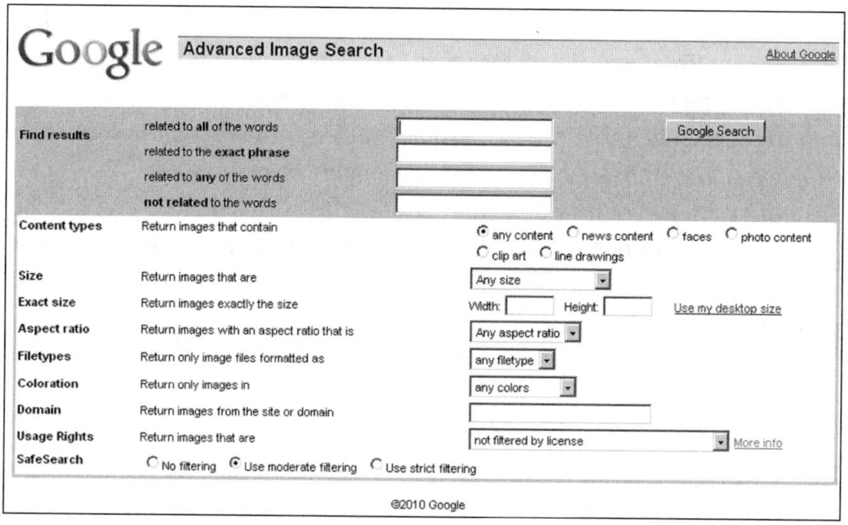

Figure 2.4 Google's Advanced Image Search

One of the key aspects of image searching in Google or another search engine is that teachers and teacher librarians need to be aware of the copyright implications of using images, for example in curricular material, which might be used within and outside the school. Teacher librarians should advise staff and students in schools about using web material such as images, so they need to study the guides provided by Google and other search engines to copyrighted material. For example, the phrase 'not filtered by license' does not mean that the user can copy an image and use it freely.

Two innovative features in Google in recent years are Google Maps and Google Earth. The maps option allows teachers to show students how to identify places on a map but can also be used to enable students to create their own maps, such as the area in which school is situated. Maps can be edited and text, photographs and video can be added. On the Google Maps home page there is an option 'My Maps', which provides the user with a guide on how to create maps. Google Earth also has many potential uses in schools and is worth exploring by teachers and teacher librarians. This tool can be used not merely to zoom in on a location in a particular country, but if used creatively can be used by teachers and teacher librarians to assist students with assignments on geography, science, history and environmental studies. Shambles.net (2010) provides a useful guide to applications for Google Earth in schools.

Google also has a news facility, which allows teachers and teacher librarians to search for news stories that might be of interest to their teaching or their students' learning. This needs careful use, however, because if the basic search is used the results may well be irrelevant. It is important to check that the news you are given comes from the country in which you are interested, for example Google News Australia. Also, there has been criticism of how up to date the results in Google News tend to be. Although this can be a useful tool for staff and students in schools, unless the advanced search facility is used, it is sometimes a better option to search particular newspaper sites.

Google Scholar and Google Books

For teachers and teacher librarians in secondary schools who are seeking to find freely available journal articles on curricular topics which they are teaching, or seeking to provide sources for senior students, the Google Scholar facility can be useful. As with the news tool in Google, using Google Scholar needs to be approached with caution, however. A search in 2010 for items on global warming using the basic search option produced only two articles dated after the year 2000. Using the Advanced Scholar Search facility allows the user to 'Return articles published between' particular dates, and a repeated search on this subject looking for articles published between 2005 and 2010 yielded a much larger number. A further note of caution with Google Scholar is that many of the articles retrieved may not be suitable for school students as they are in academic journals, thus there needs to be an element of mediation by the teacher librarian if Google Scholar is to prove useful.

The introduction of Google Books has proved to be controversial. There is an ongoing debate between authors, publishers and librarians on the one hand and Google on the other, which focuses mainly on the control that Google might have over future publishing. Google Books can provide free access to parts of books which a school cannot afford to buy or might only be available through interlibrary loan. As with other Google tools, Google Books is best used with the advanced search facility, Advanced Book Search, as this allows the user to search for books by author, title, publisher and a range of

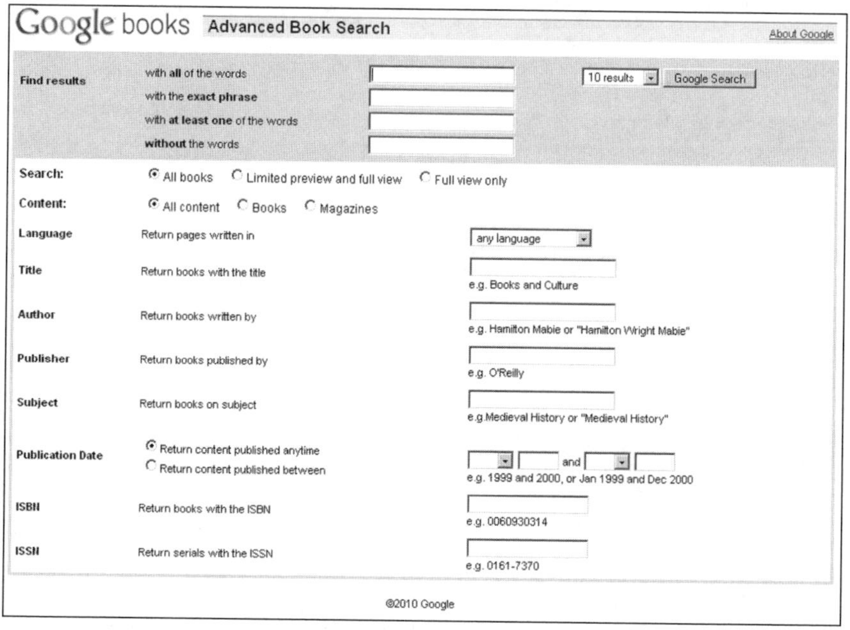

Figure 2.5 Google's Advanced Book Search

publication dates (see Figure 2.5). Even when looked at through the 'Limited view' substantial parts of the books are provided. For teachers, teacher librarians and senior students this is potentially a very powerful resource.

Metasearch engines

Google is classified as a single search engine as it searches its own database for information in relation to a user's query. There are a number of search engines that search other search engines and present what they view as the most relevant hits from these search engines. Metasearch engines include Dogpile, Excite, Info.com and Ixquick. The best known metasearch engine used in schools is Dogpile, which searches four search engines. Figure 2.6 shows the results of a search for 'tsunami causes high school' (the inclusion of 'high school' will improve the likelihood of results being relevant to high school students). In the list of results a note is given of the search engines, such as Google and Yahoo!, where the sites were found. Metasearch engines

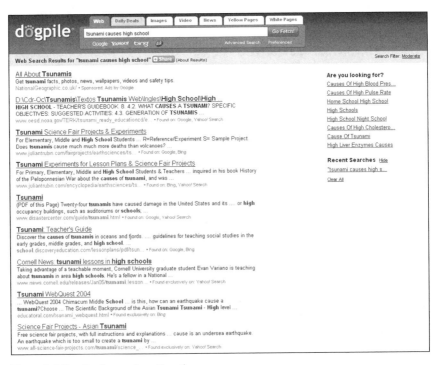

Figure 2.6 Results of a search on Dogpile

are useful because they search across other search engines and the search is therefore wider. In this author's experience, Dogpile will unearth relevant sites not found in Google. Hock (2007) agrees that metasearch engines are useful but highlights their limitations, which include the limited number of results presented from each search engine, the presence of paid listings, and the limited information on each site presented.

Visual search engines

Most search engines present their web search results in text form and it is only when performing an image search that the user is presented with visual material. One of the promised improvements in search engines in recent years is that instead of results being presented as lists, in order of relevance, users would view results in visual form, for example in a concept map or a series of screenshots from the sites listed.

A problem with visual search engines is that many promising search tools such as Kartoo and SearchMe have disappeared. The advantages of using a visual search engine are that the user can receive more information about the site before going onto it; the visual nature of the presentation makes evaluation of the sites more likely, and the visual presentation is more appealing to visual learners. In Summer 2010 the two visual search engines which appeared to be of most potential use in schools by staff and students were:

- Middlespot (http://middlespot.com), which presents a list of hits in one column and displays the web page in the main section of the page; the size of the main display can be altered, although the quality varies as size is increased.
- Viewzi (www.viewzi.com), which offers the user a series of views such as the standard text listing, the Web Screenshot view showing the site's first page, and a Google Timeline view showing the results in date order on an interactive timeline.

Visual search engines provide an alternative searching model, which may appeal to some users; visual search engines may become more common in the future.

Directories

Notess (2006, 100) defines a directory as

> a classified listing of Web sites, in which brief records for sites are placed within
> an appropriate hierarchical taxonomy. The classification of sites is typically done
> by human editors, and the sites are searchable by the category names, site titles,
> and brief site descriptions. A directory is a tool for browsing selected sites or
> getting started in a new subject area. Note that directories usually include only
> one main page per Web site.

The key aspects of this definition are that directories are designed with
human input (as opposed to machine operated search engines), are organized
hierarchically to help users identify relevant information, and are searchable.
Directories are often used for browsing rather than searching. For example, a
teacher librarian might look for 'science' in a directory and then browse
through the categories presented. Figure 2.7 shows the categories for 'science'
in the Open Directory Project (www.dmoz.org).

One directory that is particularly useful to teacher librarians is IPL2, which
is a merger of Internet Public Library and Librarians' Internet Index so, for
example, the 'Newspapers and magazines' category, when clicked, reveals
online newspapers from around the world. The best known commercial
directory is Yahoo! Directory (http://dir.yahoo.com). The question of whether
directories or search engines are the best sources of information for teachers
and teacher librarians is not particularly relevant to enhancing learning and
teaching in schools. Rather, directories should be seen as an alternative to
search engines, as they are more controlled and better organized.

Effective searching

Being an effective web searcher has a number of components, as 'effective'
may depend on the circumstances of the search. In theory, teachers and
teacher librarians will carefully think through what search words or phrases
and search tools are appropriate before they carry out a search. In practice,
time is usually a limiting factor and there is an immediate need for
information. An effective web searcher will find the most relevant and up-to-
date information in relation to an information need in the time available.

Even when time is limited, there are certain approaches to searching that will be more effective than others. People who are effective web searchers have developed a regular approach to searching, which can be seen as a set of rules or habits. Thus developing a personal approach to web searching is beneficial and one way to do this is by answering a number of questions, which will be outlined below. There are many guides to effective searching on the web, including the Berkeley Library guide (UC Berkeley Library 2009), Boswell's (2010) advice on making more effective searches, Carlson's (2002) web search 'commandments', Notess' (2006) guide to teaching web searching, and Hock's (2007) guide for experienced searchers.

The advice that follows for teachers and teacher librarians on effective web searching builds on the web guides mentioned above, focusing in particular on web searching in schools. One key aspect of searching carried out by teachers and teacher librarians is that effective searching is important for finding relevant and up-to-date information, ideas and concepts not only for

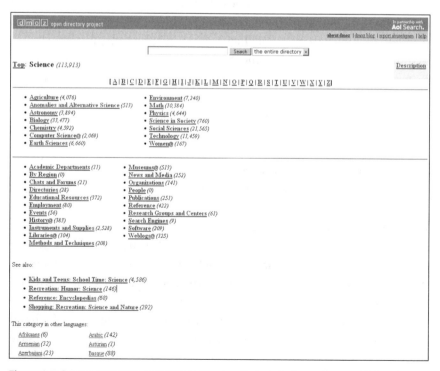

Figure 2.7 Science categories on the Open Directory Project site (www.dmoz.org/Science)

teaching and professional development, but also to enable them to pass on this experience to students, who may be faster searchers than school staff but are mostly not effective searchers.

Question 1: What am I trying to find?

This apparently simple question is, in fact, the most complex aspect of effective web searching. The question could be rephrased as 'What *exactly* am I trying to find?' For example, a teacher librarian seeking suitable sites for a teacher to use with students studying the causes and effects of tsunamis, might search for 'tsunami causes' or 'tsunami effects' in Google or another search engine and find useful results. What the teacher librarian may *exactly* be trying to find is information on the causes and effects of tsunamis but for teaching purposes, in the context of a high school.

As was stressed above, it is advisable to use the advanced search option in the user's favourite search engine in order to obtain targeted results. The teacher librarian then has two options, first to enter 'tsunami causes teaching high school' or 'tsunami effects teaching high school', thus extending the search to include 'teaching' and 'high school' in order to try to retrieve sites that are related to teaching and high schools, rather than for example material that is more suitable for university students, which would be retrieved with a more simple 'tsunami causes' search. The second and more appropriate strategy is to use the advanced search option; in Google, the teacher librarian might enter:

> *All of these words:* teaching high school
> *This exact wording or phrase:* tsunamis are caused by

Effective web searching depends on not only the choice of words or phrases used by the teacher or teacher librarian but also the quality of thinking behind these words or phrases. As noted above, advanced searching helps the user to slow down and think about what is being searched for. It is useful to write down the search terms before carrying out a search. This stops the user rushing into vague searches and creates some thinking time, which can be very useful as it is likely to result in a more effective search, and will save time later.

Question 2: What if I don't know much about the subject?

Using the advanced search option with a number of keywords or phrases is a very effective search strategy and works well when the teacher or teacher librarian has some reasonable knowledge of the topic, but there may be circumstances when this knowledge is very limited. For example, a teacher librarian helping a year 12 (final year of high school) student to find information on a project on comparing chemical and natural treatments of asthma might start a search by entering 'asthma treatment' in Google or another search engine, in order to get some ideas of how to expand this search. It might be that entering 'comparing chemical and natural treatments of asthma' in Google, or using an advanced search option and separating sections of the project title, would be effective, but where initial knowledge is sparse – and where there is time available to search in some depth – a more general approach can be effective.

Question 3: How do I stop wasting time when searching the web?

This is a very common question among school staff, although it is more often phrased as 'How do I stop *my students* wasting time when web searching?' The most obvious answer to this question is to be a more effective searcher by following the guidelines stated above in relation to thinking clearly about the search strategy and using advanced searching. In addition, teachers and teacher librarians can also consider:

- changing the focus of the search, for example by extending the search words or phrases, perhaps by adding a specific country to the tsunami examples above, or by narrowing the search terms by selecting a date range when using Google Scholar
- using a search engine such as Clusty (Clusty.com), which organizes search results into clusters and may help the searcher with alternative search word or phrases
- setting a time limit; for example if the *exact* information cannot be found in ten minutes, then seek help or use an alternative source, such as another search engine, directory or subject gateway
- saving search results; when short of time, rather than quickly searching for information and giving up, the searcher can copy the search results

from Google or another search engine, paste them into a Word document and return to the document later. The search hits can then be viewed and accessed from the Word document. Many teachers and teacher librarians, like the web using population as a whole, waste time by repeating searches unnecessarily.

Question 4: Isn't the web the best one stop shop for information for school work?

Not always. While the web can provide excellent sources of information on curricular topics and how to teach them effectively, the amount of relevant information found on the web depends on the quality of searching, the sources used (not just search engines) and the time available for searching. The issue of time is very important to teachers and teacher librarians who are often time poor because of other pressures. Reliance on the web for information often means that school staff forget about alternative sources of information, in particular people. Thus instead of spending time searching for very specific information on a new aspect of their subject topic, teachers may well often be better served by asking the teacher librarian for advice on where and how to search for this information. Similarly, teacher librarians may save time by having a second reference interview with a teacher or student, in order to find more specific information related to a query. Also, on the web itself, there are many 'Ask an expert' services and using them to post questions can serve as an alternative to further searching.

The above questions cover the main aspects of being an effective searcher, but searching is related to each individual's learning style, so although there are general guidelines for effective searching, learning what works for people as individuals is also very important. Teachers or teacher librarians can improve their individual searching effectiveness by reflecting on their search strategies and learning from successful ones.

In-service training on effective searching

Figure 2.8 shows a plan of a training programme on effective searching in schools. This could be presented by the school's teacher librarian after consultation with teaching staff and senior management. Notess (2006) observed that one of the key aspects of in-service training is that the

Effective searching: how we can use search engines for teaching and learning

Programme

9–9.15 Introduction to the session

9.15–10.15 What makes an *effective* searcher?

In this session, the group will form four sub-groups. Each sub-group will draw up a concept map (on the A3 paper provided) which identifies the key aspects of what the group considers to be *effective* searching. In drawing up the concept map, you should think about:

✓ effective searching for information on a topic that you will be teaching next term
✓ effective searching for relevant learning resources on this topic, which your students will use
✓ what advice your sub-group would give to the other sub-groups on effective searching.

The concept maps will be posted on the wall, so that all trainees can see all the concept maps. There will then be a discussion of what knowledge and skills an effective searcher might have.

[Note for trainer – not included in the programme]
This session deliberately does not focus on search engines and it leaves open the question of what sources might be used to search for information. These sources will include search web tools such as search engines, but might also include printed materials in the library and other people as sources.

10.15–10.30 Morning tea

10.30–12 noon Advanced searching in Google and other search engines

In this session . . . [the teacher librarian's name] will go through a range of features on Google, including advanced searching for different kinds of information and ideas related to your teaching and your students' learning.

[Note for trainer – not included in the programme]
The trainer will need to decide how much to include in this session. There should be time to demonstrate search engine features and for the teachers to practice, using their topics. This is an example of what might be included as part of this session.

1. Go to www.google.com.au [or equivalent in other countries] and click on 'Advanced Search'. You will see that there are many more options on this page than on the main search page. You do not have to use all of these features, but some are very useful. You can search by language, file type (for example PowerPoint), date (may be useful) and where your keywords occur (for example, in the title). We will look at the options available to you here.

We will now look at domain searching. For example, in the box 'this exact word or phrase', type in 'discovering democracy'. Now go to 'Search within a site or domain' and type in (note that you don't need www) 'det.nsw.edu.au'. Now click on the button Advanced Search. You will see that Google has returned to the 'normal' search page and in the search box you will see '"discovering democracy" site: det.nsw.edu.au'. So Google is searching for your information only in that site and nowhere else. Look at the list of sites on this topic and select the one which you think will give you most information on discovering democracy.

Figure 2.8 Extract from a training programme on effective searching for school teachers

trainer should know the audience well. One of the challenges faced in schools by teacher librarians and ICT staff is to discover the level of knowledge of, and confidence in, effective searching by teaching staff. A useful precursor to an in-service session on effective searching is to ask teachers to complete a questionnaire. This could include questions on their knowledge of search engines, searching habits and confidence in searching. It is impossible for in-service training to cover the complete range of knowledge and skills in effective searching required in any school, so the teacher librarian needs to focus carefully on what would be most beneficial to the trainees. Figure 2.8 shows what a half-day session for 12 teachers could include.

Conclusion

The increased emphasis on the use of ICT in classrooms and school libraries in schools across the world makes it imperative that teachers and teacher librarians, as well as their students, can make effective use of the web. Being able to find and use relevant information, ideas and concepts through search engines and directories should now be regarded as one of the *key* skills for teachers and teacher librarians to acquire and develop. Effective searching skills are part of a range of knowledge and skills related to information literacy in schools, and employing information literate teachers and teacher librarians will enhance the quality of teaching in the school.

References

Boswell, W. (2010) *How to Search the Web Faster, Easier, and More Efficiently*,
    http://websearch.about.com/od/searchingtheweb/tp/web_search_simple.htm.
Carlson, C. (2002) *Notes from the Trenches: the seven commandments of highly effective searching*,
    www.llrx.com/columns/notes54.htm.
Hock, R. (2007) *The Extreme Searcher's Internet Handbook: a guide for the serious searcher*, 2nd edn, Cyberage Books.
Notess, G. (2006) *Teaching Web Search Skills, Information Today*, Inc.
Shambles.net (2010) *Google Earth Lessons*,
    www.shambles.net/pages/learning/GeogP/gearthplan.

UC Berkeley Library (2009) *Finding Information on the Internet: a tutorial,*
www.lib.berkeley.edu/TeachingLib/Guides/Internet/Strategies.html.

Evaluating websites

3

Having read this chapter you will be able to:

- critically reflect on the value of a range of website evaluation criteria

- understand the crucial importance of educational criteria when evaluating websites

- evaluate websites using educational, technical and reliability criteria

- create an in-service session on website evaluation for staff in your school

Introduction

In 21st-century schools web-based resources are becoming the most common way for teachers, teacher librarians and students to access information. This chapter focuses on the need for teachers and teacher librarians to be experts in evaluating websites (Chapter 7 covers how to teach students to evaluate them). The importance of effective, as opposed to cursory, website evaluation cannot be underestimated. When teachers and teacher librarians are searching the web to find relevant websites to use in teaching, or for students to use, they will ensure that they find the best possible sites for themselves and their students by evaluating potentially useful websites.

In this chapter a range of website evaluation criteria are introduced, and some examples are critically analysed. Then the author lists his evaluation criteria for websites, which can be practically applied by school staff. The chapter ends with an example of a workshop for school staff, which can be adapted to suit local needs. Being able to evaluate websites effectively is an undervalued skill in most schools, but given the increasing use of websites in schools it should be among the core competencies of today's teachers and teacher librarians.

Website evaluation criteria
Why evaluate websites?

Brown (2002) identifies a number of reasons why teachers and teacher librarians need to evaluate websites:

◆ absence of guidelines – the web allows anyone to post any kind of information on a website
◆ absence of monitoring – there is little reviewing or editing of material posted on the web, unlike that carried out for published books
◆ lack of representation – most of the material on the web is put there by a small minority of the world's population, with many countries, in particular in Africa, lacking a web presence
◆ possibility of bias – the web allows people to add propaganda to websites, and there is much commercial material on the web, which increases the likelihood of bias.

Brown (2002) argues that the 'best form of monitoring available for teachers and students is the use of critical thinking skills and constant questioning about the validity and quality of the information being encountered on the Internet'. For teachers and teacher librarians, perhaps the most important reason for evaluating websites is that they have a professional and ethical responsibility to use the best available information they can find for their teaching and for their students to use. They should therefore take website evaluation seriously; it should be effective and not cursory. If a teacher or teacher librarian engages in cursory website evaluation, involving perhaps a brief look at a website's content and appearance, there is a danger that the use of the website will prove to be unreliable in parts and not useful for teaching or learning. When school staff evaluate websites effectively, which involves spending time applying quality website evaluation criteria, they ensure that the websites (or part of websites) they use will be fit for purpose and enhance teaching and learning with a specified group of students.

Website evaluation criteria sets

Many sets of website evaluation criteria can be found on the web in the school and university sectors. The task of monitoring this wide array of criteria sets may well fall to the teacher librarian in the school, who can profitably advise teachers of a sample of the best quality criteria to use. There is no one definitive set of website criteria, but for primary and secondary or high schools, some criteria sets are much more useful than others as they focus on, or can be applied to, the distinctive needs of teachers and students.

Schrock's (2009a) guides for school staff include a number of surveys, which can be downloaded. One of them is for teachers and teacher librarians searching for material for their own (rather than their students') use and asks users a series of questions about the content of a web page (Figure 3.1). They extend what is covered by other sets of website evaluation criteria and include questions about whether another source might provide better information or if the web page pointed the user to other online and printed information sources. It would also be useful to question whether the content of the page completely, or only partially, meets the needs of the user. The evaluation surveys suggested by Schrock could be shared among staff, and the teacher librarian might be the coordinator of these surveys, thus avoiding duplication by teachers.

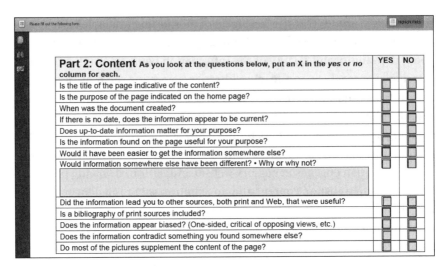

Part 2: Content As you look at the questions below, put an X in the *yes* or *no* column for each.	YES	NO
Is the title of the page indicative of the content?	☐	☐
Is the purpose of the page indicated on the home page?	☐	☐
When was the document created?	☐	☐
If there is no date, does the information appear to be current?	☐	☐
Does up-to-date information matter for your purpose?	☐	☐
Is the information found on the page useful for your purpose?	☐	☐
Would it have been easier to get the information somewhere else?	☐	☐
Would information somewhere else have been different? • Why or why not?	☐	☐
Did the information lead you to other sources, both print and Web, that were useful?	☐	☐
Is a bibliography of print sources included?	☐	☐
Does the information appear biased? (One-sided, critical of opposing views, etc.)	☐	☐
Does the information contradict something you found somewhere else?	☐	☐
Do most of the pictures supplement the content of the page?	☐	☐

Figure 3.1 Schrock's guide to evaluating websites for teachers
(http://school.discoveryeducation.com/schrockguide/pdf/evalteacher.pdf)

Schrock has produced other guides, which can be used by school staff and students, for example *The 5 Ws of Website Evaluation* (2009b). The five Ws are:

WHO: Who wrote the pages and are they an expert? Is a biography of the author included? How can I find out more about the author?

WHAT: What does the author say is the purpose of the site? What else might the author have in mind for the site? What makes the site easy to use? What information is included and does this information differ from other sites?

WHEN: When was the site created? When was it last updated?

WHERE: Where does the information come from? Where can I look to find out more about the sponsor of the site?

WHY: Why is this information useful for my purpose? Why should I use this information? Why is this page better than another?

The most important of these questions is the last one – 'Why is this information useful for my purpose?'

There are many website evaluation criteria designed by universities for their students, which are often not useful for teachers and teacher librarians because they assume a certain level of language and intellectual ability. The guides for students evaluated in Chapter 7 often try to assist students by using simple language. A typical example is one from University of Queensland Library (2008). This makes a number of important points, which teachers, in particular, might learn from, for example, that the web is not the only source of information – books and journal articles may well provide better quality information. This guide encourages users to look at a site's author, date, purpose of site, scope, writing style and language. This is a useful guide for school staff, but, as with the Schrock guide above, does not ask users to explore their purpose for evaluating a website. For example, if a teacher or teacher librarian wishes to extend their knowledge of constructivist teaching methods, they will require a site that is authoritative and provides explanations using a high level of language.

Website evaluation for teachers and teacher librarians: a guide

This author regards the key aspects of website evaluation by teachers and teacher librarians to be educational criteria, reliability criteria and technical criteria, and ideally school staff should consider them in this order.

Educational criteria

Educational criteria relate to learning and teaching in the school: what is taught (the curriculum), how it is taught (teaching methods) and what students will be learning. The main use of educational criteria is specificity – teachers and teacher librarians will not be evaluating websites in a general sense but very specifically. 'Is this site useful for this group of students, with this range of reading levels, studying this particular topic?' is the key question to address, rather than 'Does this site seem suitable for use by students?' For example, a year 9 teacher seeking sites for her students to use in exploring aspects of the possible effects of global warming on Antarctica would focus first on the site's suitability for most of the students in the class, who have an average reading ability. If the site meets this criterion, it would be selected. This would then lead the teacher to seek other, perhaps less complex, sites, which would be suitable for those with a lower than average reading ability. The teacher might then address other educational criteria, always going back to the purpose of what was being taught and what was being learned. One of the purposes of the lesson on this aspect of Antarctica might be geared towards students' use of graphs to demonstrate their understanding of climate change. The teacher would then apply the criteria relating to students studying the topic. If the first site did not meet this criterion, he or she would select another site.

Before applying educational criteria, teachers and teacher librarians might ask:

◆ What is the purpose of the lesson(s) I will be teaching?
◆ What is the range of reading levels in this class?
◆ What activities will the students be engaged in?
◆ Can I find several websites on this topic to allow for differentiation?
◆ Have I searched for material which other teachers have used on this topic?

In applying educational criteria, teachers and teacher librarians might ask:

◆ Is this site suitable for my purpose? (For example, three lessons by a history teacher on the causes of World War 2 for a year 11 class)
◆ Is the content of this site wide enough or specific enough to suit my purpose? (For example, a teacher may want the class to look at introductory information on kangaroos and their habitats (wide content) or specific aspects of the habitat of the echidna (specific content)
◆ What levels of language are used on this site? (For example, in one large site, there may be sections where non-technical language is used to explain how wind turbines work, while other sections explain the machinery of wind turbines in very technical detail)
◆ Are there activities on this site in which the students can engage? (For example, a year 8 science class studying photosynthesis would benefit from a site that asks them to take part in online experiments)
◆ Will this site motivate some or all of my students? (For example, a year 10 class studying a Shakespearean play are likely to be more engaged if they can view section of the play being enacted, or listen to interviews with actors)

◆ Is the visual material on this site important for some of my students? (For example, a class of Year 7 geography students will include many visual learners, who will be more active learners if provided with a site that is visually stimulating but also informative and challenging)
◆ Will this site extend the learning of my students? (For example, a year 5 class reading a novel about family relationships will benefit from links a fiction-related site to other sites that deal with real life family issues)

Reliability criteria

Once a site has been deemed to meet most or all of the educational criteria above, teachers and teacher librarians will need to apply further criteria to ensure that the selected site is suitable for teaching and/or learning purposes. Reliability criteria focus on the extent to which the site's information can be trusted. The Scottish Library and Information Council (SLIC) uses the term 'validity', stating, 'There are three main criteria for validating information: reliability, accuracy and currency.' SLIC defines 'reliability' as 'the expertise and reputation of those connected with the website; evidence of lack of bias; and evidence of equal emphasis towards all aspects of the search topic' (SLIC, 2006). Johnson and Lamb (2007) argue that reliability is related to the origin of the website and whether the information is likely to be accurate. They pose the following questions:

◆ Are the sources truth worthy? How do you know?
◆ Who is sponsoring this publication?
◆ Does the information come from a school, business, or company site?
◆ What's the purpose of the information resource: to inform, instruct, persuade, sell? Does this matter?
◆ What's their motive?

This author would recommend teachers and teacher librarians to use Table 3.1 when judging the reliability of websites:

Technical criteria

Almost all of the website evaluation criteria sets to be found on the web

Table 3.1 Reliability criteria for evaluating websites

Question	Key aspects of a reliable website	Example
Who produced this website?	It is clear who the author(s) is/are, e.g. an individual or an organization	The website is based in a university department
	This individual or organization be trusted, e.g. the author is a government department or a recognized person, such as an expert in the field	The author is a leading scientist in her field
	The author(s) can be contacted, if need be	There is an email contact provided
When was this site last updated?	There is a clear indication of when the website was updated and evidence of updating (be aware that it is possible to change the date of updating on the site automatically)	The 'last updated' date on the site is recent and it clearly includes new information
	Some of the information on the site may be more than 10 years old, but still very useful. There is a clear indication on the site of which information is current and which information is older	A government site has health statistics from the 1990s but also a comparison with current statistics
Is the site up to date?	The information on the site can be seen to be current. It includes references to current political, economic or social events	Media sites provide very recent political news
How accurate is the site?	The information on the site can be easily checked against other sites or from links on that site	Websites that produce claims based on surveys, e.g. for particular medical treatments
Is the site unreasonably biased?	No website is completely free of bias from some people's perspective, e.g. a government website and the opposition party's website may cover the country's economic outlook, but will come to different conclusions; the views are not unreasonably biased	A campaign group's site for a greener environment clearly identifies its aims and declares political allegiances
	Reliable sites do not display racist, sexist or extreme political views, and do not attempt to present views of others which are false	Some sites portray themselves as providing unbiased information, e.g. on Martin Luther King, but are fronts for political extremism and/or racism
Is the site trying to mislead the user?	The function of the website is very clear, e.g. it is a commercial site selling educational material, and does not pretend to be otherwise. There is no attempt to mislead the reader	Some sites advertise 'free' educational software, e.g. flowchart software. The 'free' software is either a short trial or a version which cannot be fully used

include a section on technical criteria, which comes first in many sets. This author's view is that there has been an overemphasis on technical aspects of websites and the need to provide today's students with websites that are mainly visual. Technical criteria are important, for example, if a website is very slow to load, then it is not worth pursuing. It is important, however, for teachers and teacher librarians to consider educational criteria and reliability criteria *first*, and then consider technical criteria. For example, a site which is reliable and has content which is very suitable, in level of language terms and relevance to the topic being studied by students, should not be rejected because it is technically inferior to other sites. Schrock's (2009a) critical evaluation survey for teachers addresses technical criteria and, in particular, aspects of page design and layout, graphics and photographs, and links to other sites. This author would recommend that teachers and teacher librarians pose these questions when addressing the technical features and functions of a website:

- Does the web page load in a reasonable time? (This will depend on who is using the website. If a teacher or teacher librarian is the user, slow loading may not be important. For students, it will be much more important.)
- How easy is it to navigate around the site? (If selecting the site for students, ease of navigation is important. A check should be made on whether students can get lost or distracted if they follow the links on the page.)
- Is there too much or too little text on the page? (Again, this will depend on potential users. Upper secondary or high school students should tolerate text heavy sites, whereas upper primary or lower secondary or high school students are likely to be put off by too much text.)
- Are all the graphics, and/or photos, videos and tables on the site necessary? (If there are too many non-textual elements on the website, students may become distracted by them and fail to concentrate on the key content of the site, which could be mainly in the displayed text.)
- Do all the links work? (If students are recommended by the teacher or teacher librarian to use a site with broken links, the students' willingness to use other recommended sites may be limited.)
- Is there an allowance for students with a visual handicap? (Websites

should have the facility to be viewed by all students, and the design of the website should take into account factors such as the use of colour and the hyperlink states.)

◆ Can the user find the relevant information in three clicks? (The 'three click rule' is often cited as a guide to good website design, although research by Porter (2003) suggests that it may not be as important as previously thought.)

In-service training

There is a case to be made for all teaching and school library staff to have training in website evaluation. Anecdotal evidence suggests that in most schools there is an assumption that teachers will be aware of the importance of, and the criteria for, effective website evaluation. This assumption is false: whereas teacher librarians may have covered website evaluation in their education or staff development, teachers are unlikely to have done so. Teacher librarians and teachers should argue that an in-service session on website evaluation should be a priority for the school, however much competition there is for these training sessions. They can support this claim by arguing that teachers increasingly use websites as key sources for learning and teaching; in-service training would develop teachers' competencies in this area; an improvement in website evaluation by teachers in all subjects could lead to a rise in the quality (and sharing) of resources throughout the school; and if teachers were better trained in website evaluation they could more easily pass this expertise on to their students, or reinforce website evaluation skills among them. Figure 3.2 is an example of a possible outline for an in-service session for teachers in a school. This session should be adapted to suit local circumstances.

Conclusion

Teachers and teacher librarians use web-based material more and more. There is a need to ensure that they evaluate what they find on the web effectively, given the huge variety in quality of information available. Having a school staff well versed in website evaluation and applying the criteria discussed above will go some way to ensuring that the resources they use will be closely related to their educational needs. Teachers and teacher librarians should combine effective searching on the web with effective evaluating of

---

Evaluating websites for teaching and learning: a workshop for teachers

Aims

- To allow teachers to establish a range of website evaluation criteria for use across the school
- To compare the criteria established by teachers with James Herring's educational, reliability and technical criteria
- To discuss methods of teaching students how to evaluate websites effectively, and how to reinforce these skills across the curriculum

Tasks

1. Teachers form groups of four or five, with each group consisting of a mix of subject teachers.
2. Individually, all teachers should view three websites (see below) and note down the criteria that they might use to evaluate aspects of the website. **(10 minutes)**
3. In groups, teachers should compare the criteria they have listed individually and prepare a concept map on website evaluation. The concepts maps are posted on the walls of the seminar room and teachers go round the room and read them. **(20 minutes)**
4. Each group has a short discussion on the criteria shown in the concept maps. **(5 minutes)**
5. Each group looks at James Herring's lists of educational, reliability and technical criteria, compare them with their own concept map, and draw up list of criteria which might be used across the school. **(10 minutes)**
6. There is a discussion on what might be included in a school wide list of website evaluation criteria, taking into account the concept maps and Herring's list. **(10 minutes)**

Websites

Each group should be given a list of three websites, which cover different areas of the curriculum. At least one of the websites should be related to the teachers' educational or subject knowledge (for example a site on using wikis in the classroom), with two remaining websites related to the school curriculum. The websites selected should be of variable quality and a mixture of mainly text-based sites and more visually oriented sites. All groups can evaluate the same three websites or different groups can have different websites.

Handout

A handout should accompany this session, including James Herring's list of criteria (with the source fully acknowledged), and links to website evaluation criteria such as those of Schrock or Johnson and Lamb.

Figure 3.2 Outline of an in-service training session for teachers on website evaluation

websites if they are to find and use quality learning resources for their own and their students' use.

References

Brown, J. (2002) *Why Evaluate Web Information*,
    www.ed.uiuc.edu/wp/credibility/page2.html.

Johnson, D. and Lamb, A. (2007) *Evaluating Internet Resources*,
     http://eduscapes.com/tap/topic32.htm.
Porter, J. (2003) *Testing the Three Click Rule*,
     www.uie.com/articles/three_click_rule.
Schrock, K. (2009a) *Critical Evaluation Surveys*,
     http://school.discoveryeducation.com/schrockguide/eval.html.
Schrock, K. (2009b) *The 5 Ws of Website Evaluation*,
     http://kathyschrock.net/abceval/5ws.pdf.
Scottish Library and Information Council (2006) *Validity of Information*,
     www.ictl.org.uk/U1O3CG/page_02.htm.
University of Queensland Library (2008) *Internet Resource Evaluation: how-to
     guide*,
     www.library.uq.edu.au/ssah/useits/inteval.pdf.

Web 2.0 and schools

Having read this chapter you will be able to:

- define Web 2.0 and identify a range of Web 2.0 tools
- critically evaluate the use of Web 2.0 in schools
- apply your knowledge of Web 2.0 tools in your own school
- evaluate future developments on the web
- create an in-service session on Web 2.0 for staff in your school.

Introduction

There have been many new developments on the web in the past five years, the most important of which is the development of Web 2.0, which has provided teachers and teacher librarians with a range of new concepts, ideas and tools to use in their schools. Web 2.0 has also transformed the way school students communicate with each other, and create, find and exchange information in text and visual formats inside and outside school. There has been a revolution in the way the web is used, with teachers, teacher librarians and students no longer being passive users of the web. Instead, they have become active creators of information and active respondents to information provided by others.

In the school context the existence of Web 2.0 does not guarantee that students will automatically become more effective learners or that teachers will become more effective educators. Web 2.0, in the form of blogs, wikis and other applications, has to be used as a tool that creates opportunities for learning or enhances teaching. For example, teachers who use wikis to list unannotated websites or to display the contents of handouts previously given in print are not making creative use of Web 2.0. Thus Web 2.0 needs to be seen in the learning and teaching context of the school. This chapter will examine what Web 2.0 is, and specific tools including blogs, wikis, social bookmarking, photo sharing and social networking.

What is Web 2.0?

O'Connell argues that 'Web 2.0 is fundamentally participative, and is about sharing code, content and ideas. It is about communication and facilitating community' (2006, 46). Web 2.0 refers to a new stage of development in the world wide web. Whereas the web was formerly mainly static and non-interactive, and most websites were created by businesses, universities and research institutions, Web 2.0 is seen as dynamic, interactive and much of the web activity is about sharing information and ideas. Also, new web tools such as wikis (see below) make it much easier for many more people to create web content. In short, the web has become more democratic. As Web2 tutorial states, 'The web became a two-way street. Everyday people were now creating the content. By 2007, a second generation of the web had taken over – Web 2.0. Also known as the Read/Write Web, the new web is a breeding ground for creative and engaging educational endeavours' (2008). Web 2.0

therefore provides teacher librarians and other educators with a range of tools, which can be used to improve information literacy, to provide students with access to mediated resources, to allow students to participate creatively on the web and to encourage collaboration between teacher librarians, students and teachers.

Blogs

A blog – originally called weblog – can be used for different purposes. It can be a single author blog in which one person writes all the entries and other people read them. Examples of single author blogs for teachers and teacher librarians include:

- ◆ James Herring's Blog (http://jherring.wordpress.com)
- ◆ Judy O'Connell's HeyJude (http://heyjude.wordpress.com)
- ◆ Doug Johnson's Blue Skunk Blog (http://doug-johnson.squarespace.com/)
- ◆ David Warlick's 2 Cents Worth (http://davidwarlick.com/2cents).

These blogs can be educationally informative as well as entertaining, and their value is that they provide readers with up-to-date discussion on key topics relating to schools, and particularly to the use of ICTs, including the web. Much of what appears in them can be readily used by teachers and teacher librarians. Figure 4.1 shows the HeyJude blog.

Blogs can be used by teachers and teacher librarians for a variety of purposes. Edublogs (2008) provides a list of potential uses, including:

- ◆ posting lists of resources that students can access in the library or online
- ◆ starting a discussion to which students can contribute, for example, a debate on a topical issue such as privacy
- ◆ using the blog as a library newsletter, for example, providing photographs of new books
- ◆ sharing lesson plans with other teachers, for example, the teacher librarian explaining how she teaches information literacy sessions, and how this might be reinforced in the classroom.

The book is dead - long live the book

Published Australia , eBook Readers 4 Comments
Tags: book, books, ebooks

So much is said and written about the 'demise' of the book these days. However, amongst the media hype and one-eyed negativism that sometimes abounds – there are also rational evangelists who focus on knowledge, culture and the role of digitised text in extending the possibilities for humanity.

At a recent conference hosted by the Association of Independent Schools, I encountered just such an evangelist. Sherman Young, who writes The Book is Dead blog as a companion to his book by the same title (download the first chapter), tantalized the audience with his presentation 'The Book is Dead'.

Sherman kept the **BOOK** right in perspective – both past forms and future possibilities were discussed.

Book culture is too often confused with reading culture – and it is this reading culture that Sherman explained as **'long-form' text**. A book is a process – it requires time to write and time to read. A book makes premium demands of authors and readers: a writer can reflect and dig deeper into ideas, subtly constructing reality, thereby encouraging analysis, thought, reflection. In fact, in a book the creation of a new reality is delegated to the reader.

Sherman reminded us that in fact **BOOKS HAVE BEEN DIGITAL FOR ABOUT 20 YEARS!!**

Eureka! Of course books have been digital – once we got rid of hot metal presses, and moved to typesetting then desktop publishing, all books were digital first, then adapted to be printed.

Now the digital books are getting sophisticated and devices have emerged that make them easy to read. In addition, books are being digitised the world over to share, and to facilitate learning and research. Take a look at the Rare Book Room, and think about the value of this type of easy access to our literary and knowledge heritage.

In an online world we can and have to ensure that books remain – it's about what books have done that counts. Even Google books are a way of ensuring that books survive.

Previous entries
Body in the library – a murder mystery of our own!
Metaweb adds Semantic search value!
Infowhelm
Bump your next PD!
What matters more than your talents?
Don't turn a digital blind eye...

Recent Favourites
Infowhelm
Body in the library – a murder mystery of our own!
About
Domains confusion - help anyone?
Student Tools - Let them fly!
Metaweb adds Semantic search value!

Figure 4.1 Blog of HeyJude, Australia (http://heyjude.wordpress.com)

Some blogs in schools have developed from being mainly textual postings to become interactive websites, which contain textual and visual information, and can be used by students as the basis for subject learning, skills acquisition and discussion. Figure 4.2 shows the St Andrews Lutheran College Library blog, which is hosted by the teacher librarian; students can post comments on the blog about their reading for school work or for recreation.

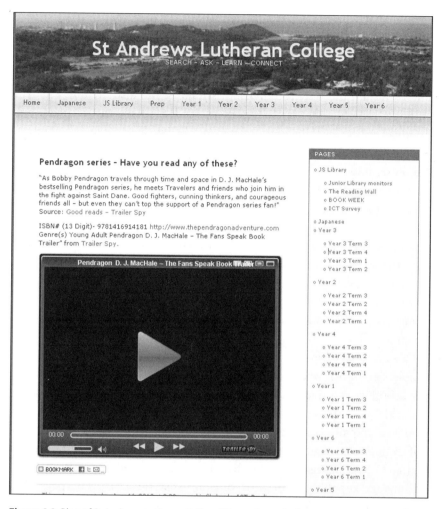

Figure 4.2 Blog of St Andrews Lutheran College Library, Australia (http://salcjs.edublogs.org/)

Wikis

Lamb and Johnson state, 'Wikis are collaboratively created web sites. . . . A wiki uses web-based open-editing tools to provide an easy way for multiple participants to enter, submit, manage, and update web pages. Wiki-based systems are popular because they are simple to install and contributors do not need special software' (2007, para 2). For teachers and teacher librarians, wikis present much greater opportunities than blogs to create learning websites for students and to involve students in their own learning.

The use of wikis in schools is limited only by the imagination of the teacher librarian or teacher who creates the wiki. Thus wikis can be used to create mediated lists of resources for students, and allow students to add resources they have found to the list. A wiki is more adaptable than a blog in that a wiki might contain not only resources for students, but also include what the students are studying, the assignment students have to complete, and information literacy skills advice to students. Wikis can include text, graphics, photographs and videos.

An example of the creative use of wikis is provided by McPherson who writes about wikis being used to encourage the development of student writing. He states, 'wikis provide students with a variety of authentic audiences, ranging from students themselves to anyone in the world with internet access. . . . Another manner in which wikis can positively enhance a student's writing experience and open possibilities for developing writing skills is by providing collaborative writing contexts' (2006, 70). Brisco (2007) provides a useful guide to choosing a wiki tool for teachers and teacher librarians, and wiki tools such as Wikispaces are discussed in more detail in Chapter 7.

One of the key aspects of wikis for teachers and teacher librarians is the simplicity of use. A wiki is basically a blank web page, which can be edited by the user. Figure 4.3 shows a wiki page created by the teacher librarian at Arendal International School in Norway. The wiki provides guidance for students, and allows students to contact the teacher librarian and to write self-evaluations. Figure 4.4 shows a wiki created by a science teacher at Marian College in Australia. As well as providing detailed information on the syllabus and key online sources for students to use, the 'Discussion' page allow students to ask questions, which the teacher answers online, thus providing all students with the answers.

Wikis can also be used as a source for school staff. An excellent example of this is the wiki at Nelson Central School, New Zealand, established as a store for ideas on using ICT in the school, and a record of what staff had done with a range of ICT tools. It provides a reference point for staff, who can check how to use Web 2.0 tools or refresh their knowledge on them. The school holds a weekly 'TechiBrekkie' session, backed up by the wiki. The wiki is particularly useful for new staff, who use it to learn about ICT, and existing staff work with new staff who are developing ICT based material in the school. One of the most laudable aspects of this wiki is that it is available on the web

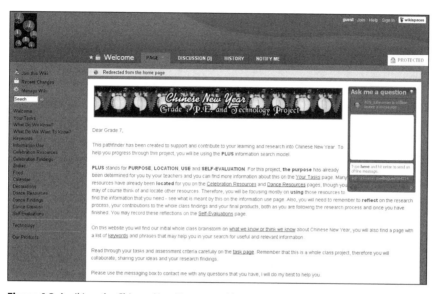

Figure 4.3 A wiki on the Chinese New Year created for year 7 at Arendal International School, Norway (http://chinesenewyearcelebration.wikispaces.com/Welcome)

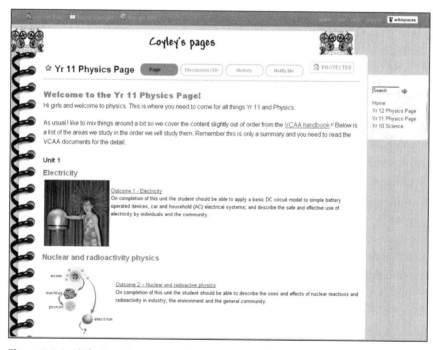

Figure 4.4 A wiki for Year 11 science students at Marian College, Australia (http://coyleyspages.wikispaces.com/Yr+12+Physics+Page)

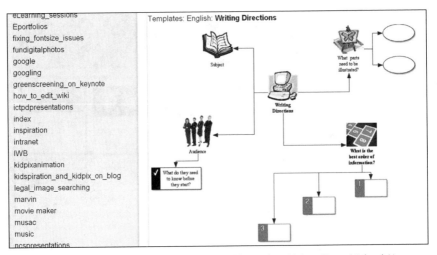

Figure 4.5 Advice on using 'Inspiration' from the staff ICT wiki at Nelson Central School, New Zealand (http://nelsoncentral.wikispaces.com/inspiration)

(http://nelsoncentral.wikispaces.com) for other schools across the world to use. Figure 4.5 shows part of a guide to using 'Inspiration' on the school's ICT wiki.

Social bookmarking

O'Connell states that 'Social bookmarking, using such tools as Del.icio.us make it possible to track websites, annotate websites and add keywords (tags) to categorize information. Forget the confusion of bookmarking websites on your own computer, ordered only by folders ' (2006, 47). Social bookmarking is another collaborative or sharing feature of Web 2.0 and can be useful in searching for websites identified by others. Steffens (2008) focuses on Diigo (www.diigo.com) and outlines the ways in which teachers and teacher librarians can upload bookmarked sites to Diigo, where they are saved. The advantages of social bookmarking are that access to bookmarked sites is not restricted to one computer in the school, and bookmarked sites can be tagged by the user for later retrieval. Steffens states, 'For example, you can tag all of the sites that are helpful to students about geometry, and then the websites for data analysis or the bookmarks for the unit on Greek mythology' (2008).

In Troy High School, USA, the teacher librarian works closely with teachers and students in using social bookmarking sites such as Sqworl

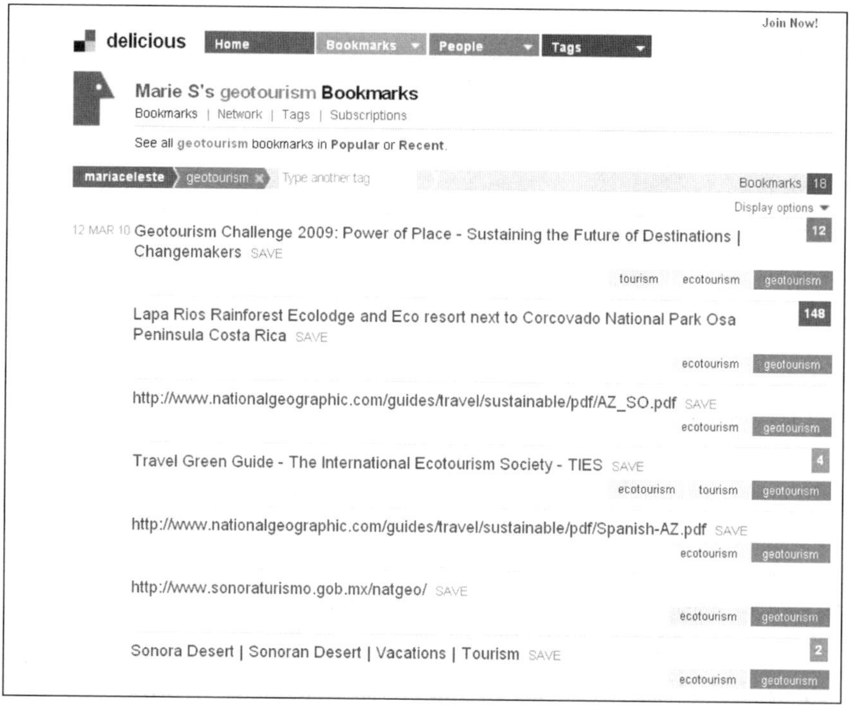

Figure 4.6 Social bookmarking for students studying geotourism at Troy High School, USA (www.delicious.com/mariaceleste/geotourism)

(http://sqworl.com), Diigo and Delicious (http://delicious.com). Figure 4.6 shows an example of bookmarked sites for a teacher of Spanish who was seeking sites related to geotourism in Spanish speaking countries. In this school, the teacher librarian uses Delicious not only to bookmark her own sites, but also to learn from others who have bookmarked sites on particular topics. The teacher librarian and teachers in the school recognize that having mediated resources available for students enables these students to focus more on their topics and waste less time in fruitless searching. They encourage students to become involved in bookmarking and to add annotations to the sites which are being bookmarked when carrying out project work.

Podcasting

Eash describes a podcast as 'a digital audio file that's created, shared, and heard' (2006). Teachers and teacher librarians use podcasts – audio

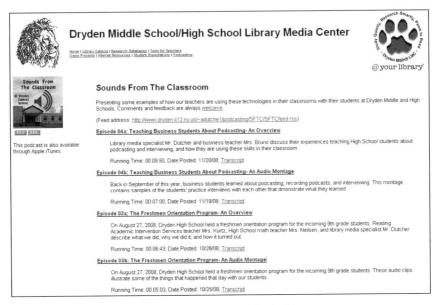

Figure 4.7 Examples of podcasting at Dryden Middle School, USA
(www.dryden.k12.ny.us/~adutche1/podcasting/SFTC/index.htm)

broadcasts, using software such as Audacity (http://audacity.
sourceforge.net), which are saved as mp3 files and can be listened to on a
computer, laptop or mp3 playing device – to add value to their teaching.
Podcasts allow students to listen to the recordings in any place that has access
to a PC, laptop or mp3 playing device. They can listen more than once and in
various positions, for example while sitting in front of a PC or laptop, or while
travelling in a train or car. Figure 4.7 shows an example of how teachers and
the teacher librarian collaborated to use podcasts at Dryden Middle School.

Photo sharing

There are a number of photo sharing sites on the web including Picasa
(http://picasa.google.com) and Flickr (www.flickr.com). These sites can host
photographs sent in by individuals or by organizations such as schools, and
while the sites are mainly used for recreational purposes, they can be a very
useful source of material for use by students. Figure 4.8 shows Flickr's
Creative Commons (www.flickr.com/creativecommons), which provides a
repository of over 20 million photographs. They can be found and used under
the Attribution License, which allows students and staff in schools to use the

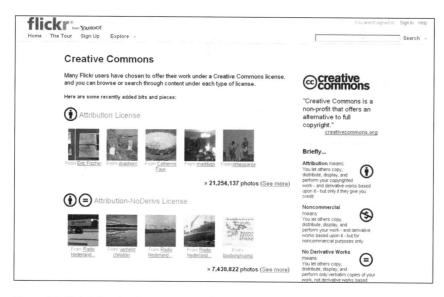

Figure 4.8 Flickr's Creative Commons (www.flickr.com/creativecommons); reproduced with permission of Yahoo! Inc. (c)2010 Yahoo! Inc.; Flickr and the Flickr logo are registered trademarks of Yahoo! Inc.

photos they have retrieved, as long as they acknowledge the source of the photos. Although Flickr is mainly a site for social photographs, a search for 'volcanoes' on Flickr revealed a number of photos from NASA, including shots of the Icelandic volcano which erupted in 2010. Thus teachers and teacher librarians who are creating resources for students can include accredited photos in the knowledge that they are not breaking copyright. Flickr's Creative Commons site can also be used by teachers and teacher librarians to teach students about copyright.

VoiceThread

VoiceThread (http://voicethread.com) is a multimedia tool, which can be used in schools to encourage discussion or debate about topics. It allows users to post a text document, graphic, photograph or video, which can then be commented on by others, so can clearly be used effectively by teaching staff in schools. Students can contribute to discussions in text, audio or video form and their 'comments' can be in the form of creative material such as pictures or poems. Figure 4.9 shows how VoiceThread is used by an art teacher at Robert Usher Collegiate, Canada, to encourage students to think about

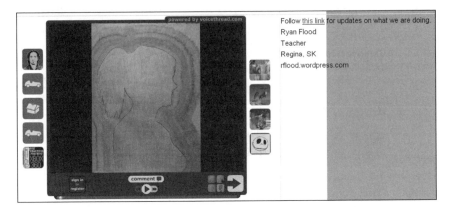

Figure 4.9 Use of VoiceThread by an art teacher at Robert Usher Collegiate, Canada
(http://voicethread4education.wikispaces.com/9-12)

emotion through colour and to produce an Expressionist self portrait, which is commented on by the teacher and other students in the icons at the side of the portrait. When clicked, these icons can be viewed as text or in audio form. VoiceThread is a commercial product, and its cost may limit its use in many schools.

Other aspects of Web 2.0

There are no agreed parameters of Web 2.0 and new applications are regularly appearing which can be used in schools. One indistinct area is social networking, which includes sites such as MySpace (www. myspace.com), Facebook (www.facebook.com) and Bebo (www.bebo.com), but may include sites like Flickr. At present, the use of social networking sites in schools is limited, but discussion continues about how they might be used to advantage.

Conclusion

The use of Web 2.0 by teacher librarians across the world is increasing daily. Issues related to the use of Web 2.0 by teacher librarians include:

◆ the time taken to develop resources
◆ the availability of in-service training for teacher librarians

♦ access to Web 2.0 sites, some of which may be blocked by the school's firewall.

Despite this, Web 2.0 is an exciting challenge for teacher librarians and an excellent to improve information literacy, provide resources and collaborate with teachers.

References

Brisco, S. (2007) Which Wiki Is Right for You?, *School Library Journal*, www.schoollibraryjournal.com/article/CA6438167.html.

Eash, E. (2006) Podcasting 101 for K-12 Librarians, *Information Today*, www.infotoday.com/cilmag/apro6/eash.shtml.

Edublogs (2008) *Ways to Use Your Edublog*, http://edublogs.org.

Lamb, A. and Johnson, B. (2007) *An Information Skills Workout: wikis and collaborative writing*, http://eduscapes.com/hightech/spaces/collaborative/wikiTL.pdf.

McPherson, K. (2006) Wikis and Literacy Development, *Teacher Librarian*, **34** (2), 70–2.

O'Connell, J. (2006) Engaging the Google Generation through Web 2.0, *Scan*, **25** (3), 46–50.

Steffans, P. (2008) *Diigo – 21st Century Tool for Research, Reading and Collaboration*, www.amphi.com/~technology/techtalks/online/nov08/bestpract.htm.

Web2 tutorial (2008) *Web 2.0 Tutorial*, http://web2tutorial.wikispaces.com.

5

Information literacy

Having read this chapter you will be able to:

- understand the concept of information literacy
- critically evaluate a range of information literacy skills models
- develop an information literacy programme for your school
- reflect on the issues relating to the transfer of information literacy skills and abilities
- collaborate with colleagues in developing information literate students
- plan and implement an in-service course on information literacy in your school.

Introduction

Information literacy has been recognized as one of the key abilities which people in society should have for the 21st century. Because of the rapid expansion of technology and the ever growing amount of complex information (in a range of formats), which students, school staff and the general population need to review, select, evaluate and use effectively, information literacy is one of the fundamental aspects of education for today's students. As will be seen below, there is no agreed definition of information literacy, and aspects of information literacy in schools are often referred to, for example by teachers, as study skills, research skills, media literacy and digital literacy. The term 'information literacy' is now being used more widely than it was at the end of the 20th century and can be seen in reports in the areas of business, education and ICT in society.

There have been debates in recent years about the nature of school students, who are referred to by Prensky (2009) as digital natives, and the argument of Prensky and others is that because today's students have grown up with technology and digital information, they are innately better at finding and using information, particularly from the web. This is a very debatable view, given the anecdotal evidence from schools and research studies, which show that, although a minority of students may be effective web users, most students lack the essential skills and abilities in this area. While today's students may be excellent *finders* of information, they are often found to be ineffective at finding *relevant* information. The need to develop students who can understand, use and reflect on information literacy skills is a key challenge for teachers and teacher librarians.

This chapter will examine definitions of information literacy; evaluate information literacy models; discuss the issues relating to the transfer of information literacy skills and abilities; focus on collaboration between teachers and teacher librarians in teaching information literacy; and provide examples of in-service sessions for staff, which could be used in a primary or secondary school.

Definitions of information literacy

There are many definitions of information literacy and the questions posed by Langford are still relevant today: 'Is it [information literacy] a concept or a process? . . . Or is it a new literacy that has been transformed from existing literacies to complement the emerging technologies for which the Information Age students must be skilled?' (1998). The present author defines information literacy as 'a critical and reflective ability to exploit the current information environment, and to adapt to new information environments; and as a practice'.

This definition views information literacy as an ability and a practice, rather than a set of skills (for example information retrieval skills) that students use inside and outside school. Information literacy is a critical and reflective ability. Students who engage, in web searching, for example, should be taught to use a set of skills in a critical way, to think about which skills to use and to reflect on why they might use particular skills. Then they will be effective practitioners. A further aspect of this definition, which is not included in other definitions, is the reference to new information environments – students will have the ability to transfer information literacy skills and abilities from one learning environment to another.

The implications of this definition of information literacy for teachers and teacher librarians is that there needs to be a shift in emphasis in schools from teaching students a set of skills, such as to define purpose or develop a search strategy. If students are to develop as effective information practitioners, then they need to be given the opportunity to reflect not merely on how to use certain skills, but on why they might use particular skills. There is a tendency in schools to assume that if students are taught skills such as concept mapping, they will reflect on the use of these skills and transfer them. Recent research by this author shows that this is unlikely to happen, apart from by a small minority of high achieving students. New strategies are therefore needed, which are discussed below.

Information literacy models

There are many information literacy models available for use in schools, and the most commonly used ones are the Big 6 model (Eisenberg and Berkowitz 2010), the PLUS model (Herring 1996 and 2004) and the information search process (ISP) model (Kuhlthau 2004). In Australia, the model of New South Wales, Department of Education and Training (2007a) is widely used. The Big 6 and PLUS models are actively used by students; the ISP model is used more by teachers and teacher librarians to design scaffolds for their students.

The use of information literacy models can be viewed in two ways. First, a model can be viewed as a tool for students to use and follow, which is how most models have been used in schools. Second, existing models such as Big 6 and PLUS may be seen as guides for students to develop their own model of how they define the purpose of, find and effectively use information. If teachers and teacher librarians can develop ways of encouraging students to develop their own model, then these students are more likely to be effective practitioners of information literacy skills and more effective users of digital information, including the web.

The Big 6 model

The Big 6 model is considered to be the most used model, particularly in North American schools. The six steps in the model can be seen in Figure 5.1. It takes students through a range of steps from identifying why they need information (task definition) to reflecting on how well they have used the model (evaluation). Wolf, Brush and Saye (2003) suggested that the Big 6 model could be used as a scaffold which would encourage students to engage in metacognition, as 'it provides a structured vocabulary that students and teachers can use while discussing the problem-solving strategies being employed in a particular learning situation'.

The Big 6 model at Lincoln High School, USA

The Big 6 model is used with a wide range of students at Lincoln High School, USA, who are introduced to the model in grade 7. Students are encouraged to use the school library's research guide, which provides an outline of the

1. Task definition 1.1 Define the information problem 1.2 Identify information needed	2. Information seeking strategies 2.1 Determine all possible sources 2.2 Select the best sources	3. Location and access 3.1 Locate sources (intellectually and physically) 3.2 Find information within sources
4. Use of information 4.1 Engage (e.g. read, hear, view, touch) 4.2 Extract relevant information	5. Synthesis 5.1 Organize from multiple sources 5.2 Present the information	6. Evaluation 6.1 Judge the product (effectiveness) 6.2 Judge the process (efficiency)

Figure 5.1 The Big 6 model (www.big6.com/what-is-the-big6)

Big 6 model, and extended advice on information seeking strategies, and to use the web effectively by planning searches carefully and using guidance given on website evaluation. There is also guidance on note-taking, organization of information and citation.

The Big 6 model has been used at Lincoln High School for many years and teachers and the teacher librarian have much experience in using the model with students across the curriculum. One example is students preparing for the English 4 Research Paper assignment, which the teacher librarian collaborates on and co-teaches with English Department colleagues. Students work in the Library for five class periods (90-minutes in length) on a block schedule, and use the Big 6 to guide their use of the web and the school library's databases.

The ISP model

The information search process (ISP) model was designed by Kuhlthau (2004) following a series of research studies among school students and workplace employees. It has recently been incorporated into the Guided Enquiry (Kuhlthau, Maniotes and Caspari, 2007) teaching methodology. The elements of the ISP can be seen in Figure 5.2. One of the key differences between the ISP model and other models is that Kuhlthau (2004) focused on how students were feeling at different stages of information seeking, and this is reflected in the model.

1. Initiating a research assignment Feelings: apprehension, uncertainty	2. Selecting a topic Feelings: confusion, sometimes anxiety, brief elation, anticipation
3. Exploring information Feelings: confusion, uncertainty, doubt, sometimes threat	4. Formulating a focus Feelings: optimism, confidence inability to complete task
5. Collecting information Feelings: realization of extensive work to be done, confidence in ability to complete task, increased interest	6. Preparing to present Feelings: sense of relief, sometimes satisfaction, sometimes disappointment
7. Assessing the process Feelings: sense of accomplishment or sense of disappointment	

Figure 5.2 The ISP model (From http://virtualinquiry.com/inquiry/ips.htm)

The ISP model at Gill St Bernard's School, USA

At Gill St Bernard's School, USA, there is ongoing collaboration between the teacher librarians and teachers in different parts of the curriculum, especially in science. The ISP model is introduced to students over a period of time, as part of the classes in which they are learning scientific topics and conducting research assignments. Schmidt, Kowlaski and Nevins (2010) reported on the use of the ISP model with 11th grade students and found that those who used elements of the model gained a greater understanding of using scientific literature to learn more about topics in biology, chemistry, physics and psychology. Students in this school are encouraged to provide feedback to teachers and teacher librarians on effective ways to gain new knowledge and research scientific topics. Students give feedback, for example on how to select a topic, identify relevant literature and analyse the content of digital and print resources. The teachers and teacher librarians hold tutorials to discuss potential difficulties such as uncertainty about a topic, confusion when selecting relevant sources, or information overload.

The teachers and teacher librarians encourage students in all grades to use the ISP as part of their overall learning as they believe that teaching information literacy is an integral part of the curriculum. Therefore students use the ISP model elements not just to find information for assignments, but also to develop deeper learning in curricular areas such as science. Collaboration between teachers and teacher librarians is seen as a prerequisite for the successful development of the ISP model across the school.

NSW DET model

Figure 5.3 shows the model developed for schools in New South Wales, which is designed to provide teachers and teacher librarians with a guide to developing information literacy in schools, aligned to the state's Quality Teaching Programme (NSW DET, 2006). The steps in the model, from 'Defining' to 'Assessing', identify what questions students might ask and give guidance on what skills student should have. The poster for the model (NSW DET, 2007b) is widely used in schools across the state and elsewhere in Australia.

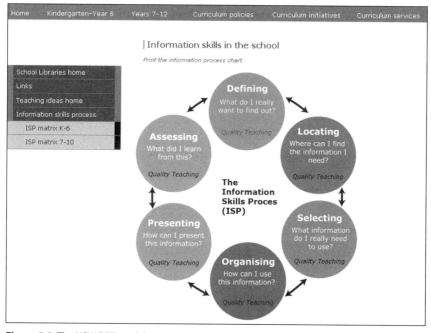

Figure 5.3 The NSW DET model
(www.curriculumsupport.education.nsw.gov.au/schoollibraries/teachingideas/
isp/index.htm)

The NSW DET model at Queenwood Junior School, Australia

The NSW DET model is used at Queenwood Junior School, Australia, an independent primary school, to support the development of information literacy across the school. The teacher librarian works with all teachers in the school and a poster of the model is in all classrooms. A recent study by Herring and Bush (2009) focused on using the model in the classroom and library. Student use of the model's elements became more effective when concepts such as 'Defining' and 'Selecting' were explained in the classroom and in the library. The study concluded that establishing a culture of transfer in the school was essential if students were to view the model as an integral part of their learning, and use the tool when completing assignments. Teachers and the teacher librarian have noted that students' use of the web, in particular their definition of purpose, has improved after using the model as a scaffold. Students in this school are now less likely to search aimlessly for material on Google. Figure 5.4 shows an example of guidance given to students on website evaluation.

NATURAL DISASTERS
Internet Resources

Title: _____

Address: _____

Author: _____

Headings on this website:

Evaluation: (circle)
This website has a useful home page.   Yes No
This website has links.   Yes No
This website contains useful illustrations and diagrams.   Yes No
I could understand the words being used on website.   Yes No
It explained what causes this natural disaster.   Yes No
It explained what happens when this natural disaster occurs.   Yes No
It explained the results / aftermath of this natural disaster.   Yes No
This author is a reliable source.   Yes No

Two interesting facts I found on this website:

I would consider this website to be: (circle)

extremely useful   useful   useful in some parts   not useful at all

Figure 5.4 Website evaluation advice to students at Queenwood Junior School, Australia

Queenwood Junior School has also found that sharing a common terminology from the elements of the NSW DET model across the school has helped teachers in particular to reinforce use of the model across the curriculum. They found this led to students using the model in different curricular areas and classrooms, as well as in the school library.

PLUS model

This author's PLUS model has been used in schools in the UK, Australia, New Zealand and South Africa. The elements of the model – purpose, location, use and self-evaluation – can be seen in more detail in Figure 5.5. Studies of the model (Herring and Tarter, 2007) have shown that most students saw

Purpose	• Identifying an information need • Learning to frame realistic research questions • Planning a piece of research using diagrams or headings • Identifying keywords
Location	• Selecting suitable information media • Locating information using library catalogues, indexes, databases, CD-ROMs or search engines
Use	• Evaluating quality and relevance of information retrieved • Skimming and scanning text for information • Taking notes • Presenting and communicating information • Writing a bibliography
Self-evaluation	• Reflecting on what has been learnt and being able to come to a conclusion based on information found • Carrying out a personal information skills audit • Identifying successful information skills strategies

Figure 5.5 James Herring's PLUS model (adapted from www.ltscotland.org.uk/5to14/specialfocus/informationskills/plus.asp)

clear benefits in using it, as it helped students to be clearer about the purpose of information needed, to find and evaluate pertinent information, to be better organized, and to reflect on their use of the information literacy skills in the PLUS model.

The PLUS model at Ripon Grammar School, UK

Students are introduced to the PLUS model in their first year at Ripon Grammar School (Year 7), a state secondary school, and encouraged to use the model in later years. Herring (2010a) found that students in year 12 had developed their own models of information literacy, using the PLUS model as the basis for developing it. The teacher librarian works closely with teachers across the curriculum, particularly in science, geography and history subjects. Handouts, also available online, provide guidance on defining a clear purpose; finding relevant information from a range of sources, including the web; effectively using information and ideas; and writing assignments. Use of the PLUS model in the school has increased students' focus on learning more about the topics they are studying and helped them with assignments on the topic. The teacher librarian and teachers use the Inspiration software (www.inspiration.com); an example of scaffolding for students using the 'Purpose' element of PLUS is shown in Figure 5.6.

Information literacy and transfer

Although there has been much discussion of and research on a range of aspects of information literacy in school, one of the underlying assumptions made about students and information literacy skills is that students will transfer skills and abilities across the curriculum and over time. Thus information literacy is often referred to as part of students' lifelong learning and there is an assumption that students will transfer skills and abilities learned in school to higher education or the workplace. Such assumptions have rarely been tested, and research carried out by this author has shown that they are false for most students.

In a recent study of three secondary or high schools in Australia, Herring (2010b) found that although year 7 (first year high school) students believed in transferring skills and abilities, such as concept mapping, question formulation, search strategy development and evaluation of information, most students did not actually transfer these skills and abilities. The research showed that there were three groups of students:

◆ actual transferrers – a minority of students who transferred skills and abilities and were able to reflect on the value of transferring them to new learning situations
◆ propositional transferrers – the majority of students who saw transfer as valuable but were reluctant or did not transfer skills and abilities
◆ non-transferrers – a very small minority of students who failed to understand the concept of transfer, and did not transfer skills and abilities.

The research also found that teachers and teacher librarians in these schools advocated transfer as a key element of learning and teaching in the school. The staff also acknowledged that there was no culture of transfer in the schools, so transfer was not directly encouraged. The practical implications for teachers and teacher librarians are that, if assumptions are made about transferring information literacy skills and abilities, but students do not transfer such skills and abilities, many students will fail to use key aspects of information literacy such as concept mapping or question formulation.

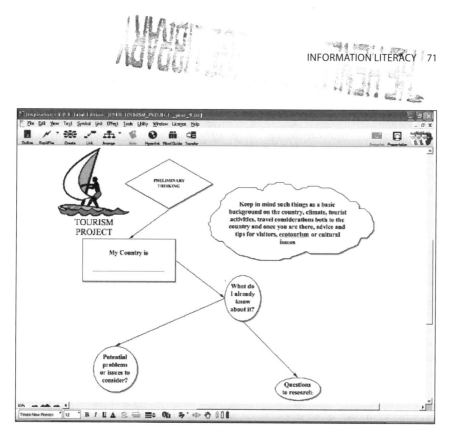

Figure 5.6 Using Inspiration with the PLUS model at Ripon Grammar School, UK

Developing a culture of transfer for information literacy in schools involves discussions about transfer and information literacy at whole school staff meetings; the development of a policy on transfer within the school; and, most importantly, concerted practice among teachers and teacher librarians to reinforce information literacy skills and abilities across the curriculum. This practice will include discussing the concept with transfer with students at all levels.

Collaboration between teachers and teacher librarians

One of the key factors in developing successful information literacy programmes in schools is collaboration between teachers and teacher librarians. Markless argues that 'When collaborating, we go beyond informing. We begin . . . in different places in our understanding . . . but gradually meanings are negotiated. Then, at some point, inspiration enters' (2009, 125). An excellent example of teacher–teacher collaboration can be seen in St George's School, Montreal. Holmes and Tobin (2005) evaluated their own collaboration and identified key elements of collaboration as being willing to listen and exchange ideas, to learn from another professional, to plan together and debrief together, and to focus on improving student learning.

Collaboration between teachers and teacher librarians to encourage information literacy in schools can take many forms. The following is a list of key activities to develop successful collaboration:

◆ Identify a common interest, for example students' use of Google.
◆ Discuss terminology. For example, the teacher librarian might use the term 'search strategy', while the teacher may simply use the term 'searching'.
◆ Discuss the learning focus. For example, the teacher should explain the learning context of Google use, which might be an assignment on climate change.
◆ Be open about what you know and what you don't know. The teacher(s) and teacher librarians should be able to ask even simple questions.
◆ Jointly plan activities for students. This may involve designing a handout or web page for students which guides their use of Google.
◆ Follow through on collaboration; have a debriefing session on how successful the planned activities and student materials were.
◆ Let other staff know what you are doing.

In-service training on information literacy

Designing an in-service course for teachers in a school needs to take into consideration the needs of the particular school, and the prior knowledge that teachers have. Following on from the collaboration discussion above, it would be profitable if an in-service session on information literacy is planned jointly by teachers and the teacher librarian so it is related to learning and teaching in the school, and not library oriented. It is likely that an in-service session on aspects of information literacy will be only part of a school's one day in-service course. Planning for specific sessions lasting no more than 60–90 minutes each is therefore advisable. They might be on information literacy, searching the web and teaching students to use websites.

Information literacy: what is it and why is it important?

This session would take the form of an introduction to the concept of information literacy and information literacy skills, and give examples of information literacy guidance for students. A joint PowerPoint presentation by a teacher and a teacher librarian would outline these aspects of information literacy. It would contain key questions for the rest of the session relating to the terminology used by different teachers, for example study skills or research skills, the experiences of teachers' observations of students using techniques such as concept mapping, and outline plans for developing more information literate students.

Searching the web: becoming a better Google user

This would be a practical session for teachers who feel that they are not effective searchers. Material from Chapter 3 of this book would be useful. A good way to start this session would be to focus on teachers developing sound search strategies. Then part of the session would not involve computer use, but would be an exercise where teachers brought a topic with them, designed a search strategy, compared their strategy with others, and noted the main elements of search strategy design. The second part of the session would be practical, with the session leader(s) taking teachers through aspects of Google and other search engines.

Teaching students to read websites

This author has run sessions with teachers and teacher librarians using the following aims and methodology.

Aims:

◆ to explore ways of teaching students how to 'read' a website
◆ to examine ways of getting student feedback on their use information skills.

Methodology:

1   Each group should discuss how they might plan a lesson(s) on teaching students how to 'read' a website effectively to increase their learning in a particular area. Each group should design a concept map which includes

the topic to be studied and the aims of the lesson, the outcomes of the lesson, the skills which the students will be taught, and hints and tips for students.

2 Each group posts their concept map on the wall for other groups to read. We discuss the implications of teaching students how to 'read' a website.

3 We discuss ways of gaining feedback on information skills from students.

In-service training sessions need to be carefully planned and teachers and teacher librarians who design such sessions should consider pre-planning aspects such as the location of the session, the equipment to be used (for example a projector linked to PC or laptop, or an interactive white board), the timing of each part of the session (for example 5 minutes introduction and 15 minutes on search strategies), and pre-session information to participants (an outline of the session and topic examples). It is vital to rehearse the session. Providing in-service sessions can be a very useful start to successful collaboration in schools.

Conclusion

Information literacy is a key component of 21st-century education. It can be seen to include other literacies such as digital literacy, visual literacy and media literacy as information is a common component of all of them. Developing students who can use their information literacy skills and abilities to harness the multitude of concepts, ideas and information on the web, and thus increase their learning, is one of the main challenges facing teachers and teacher librarians in today's schools. These professionals need to become effective information literacy practitioners themselves first, if they are then to guide students to become more alert when using the web.

References

Eisenberg, M. and Berkowitz, B. (2010) *The Definitive Big 6 Workshop Handbook*, 4th edn, Paw Prints.

Herring, J. (1996) *Teaching Information Skills in Schools*, Library Association Publishing.

Herring, J. (2004) *The Internet and Information Skills: a guide for teachers and school librarians*, Facet Publishing.

Herring, J. (2010a) Year 12 Students' Use of Information Literacy Skills: a constructivist grounded analysis. In Lloyd, A. and Talja, S. (eds) *Practising Information Literacy: bringing theories of learning, practice and information literacy together*, Centre for Information Studies, Charles Sturt University.

Herring, J. (2010b) *School Students, Question Formulation and Issues of Transfer: a constructivist grounded analysis*, Libri, in press.

Herring, J. and Bush, S. (2009) Creating a Culture of Transfer for Information Literacy Skills in Schools. In Ainsworth, A., Crothers, G., Lopez, C., Pritchard, M. and Scott, C. (eds) *Engage explore celebrate: ASLA XXI Biennial Conference Proceedings 2009*.

Herring, J. and Tarter, A. (2007) Progress in Developing Information Literacy in a Secondary School Using the PLUS Model, *School Libraries in View*, **23**, 23–7.

Holmes, A. and Tobin, E. (2005) Motivation Through Collaboration at St George's School of Montreal, *School Libraries in Canada*, **25** (2), www.clatoolbox.ca/casl/slic/SLICVol25issue2.pdf.

Kuhlthau, C. (2004) *Seeking Meaning: a process approach to library and information services*, 2nd edn, Libraries Unlimited.

Kuhlthau,K., Maniotes, L. and Caspari, A. (2007) *Guided inquiry: learning in the 21st century*, Libraries Unlimited.

Langford, L. (1998) Information Literacy: a clarification, *School Libraries Worldwide*, **4** (1), 59–72.

Markless, S. (ed.) (2009) *The Innovative School Librarian*, Facet Publishing.

New South Wales, Department of Education and Training (2006) *About Quality Teaching*, https://www.det.nsw.edu.au/proflearn/areas/qt/qt.htm.

New South Wales, Department of Education and Training (2007a) *Information Skills in the School*, www.curriculumsupport.education.nsw.gov.au/schoollibraries/teachingideas/ isp/index.htm.

New South Wales, Department of Education and Training (2007b) *Information Skills in the School*, www.curriculumsupport.education.nsw.gov.au/schoollibraries/teachingideas/ info_skills/assets/infoprocesscycle.pdf.

Prensky, M. (2009) H. Sapiens Digital: from digital immigrants and digital natives to digital wisdom, *Innovate*, **5** (3), www.innovateonline.info/index.php?view=article&id=705.

Schmidt, R., Kowlaski, V. and Nevins, L. (2010) Guiding the Inquiry Using the
    Modified SLR, *School Libraries Worldwide*, **16** (1), 13–32.
Wolf, S., Brush, T., and Saye, J. (2003) The Big Six Information Skills as a
    Metacognitive Scaffold: a case study, *School Library Media Research*, 6.
    www.ala.org/ala/aasl/aaslpubsandjournals/slmrb/slmrcontents/volume62003/
    bigsixinformation.htm.

Improving student use of the web

Having read this chapter you will be able to:

- improve the way your students plan before using the web
- improve your students' search strategies
- improve the way your students evaluate websites and the information and ideas within them
- improve the way your students read for information and interpret what they find on the web
- improve the way your students use web information and ideas as learners and when completing assignments
- teach your students to be reflective users of the web
- teach your students how to develop their own, personal model of web use.

Introduction

Using the web for school work is now an integral part of the modern student's life. The web is the first port of call if students need information for subject learning or for an assignment. Outside school, the web is also the key information source for most students, although not all students have web access at home. As the web is now such a large part of many students' lives, it is surprising that, in most schools, little time is allocated to teaching students how to be not only web users, but web learners. A web user is a person who uses the web, but this use may be superficial, mainly technical and involve little or no reflection. If students are to be *web learners*, they will develop effective search strategies (derived from an analysis of their purpose), critically evaluate what they find on the web, select information that is relevant to their purpose, use information and ideas found on the web ethically and effectively, and will learn from each use of the web, by reflecting on what they found, and how they found it. In most schools, there is an assumption that students will be web learners as well as web users, but there is little evidence of this, either anecdotally or in the research literature (Herring, 2010; Kuiper, Volman and Terwel, 2008).

To develop students from being web users to web learners, there needs to be a focus on teaching web learning skills to students, and to reinforce these skills across the school curriculum. If schools can develop an integrated approach to web learning, there is an opportunity for students to extend their use of information literacy skills and abilities and develop their own model of information literacy.

This chapter seeks to provide teachers and teacher librarians with ideas and examples for teaching students how to improve their use of the web. Most students need to be provided with scaffolding, which will help them to use the web effectively and to reflect on that use. The chapter focuses on key aspects of information literacy, which relate to students' use of the web, including planning for web searching, using effective search strategies, evaluating websites and web-based information, reading for information, reflecting on web use, and developing a personal model for web use.

Planning for web searching

One of the main criticisms of students' use of the web in schools by teachers and teacher librarians is that students tend to go straight to a search engine, most likely Google, when they need information, and waste much time in fruitless searching. Recent research by this author showed that in all three schools studied, there was criticism of students by their peers. In one school, a group of students being interviewed identified other students as failing to plan, with one student commenting 'There are some that just want to get it over and done with, so they don't think about getting the best information. They just rush into Google and look up anything.' Similar sentiments were gained from the teachers and teacher librarians. Students therefore need guidance on thinking about what they are searching for and why they are searching.

The information literacy models discussed in Chapter 5 all contain aspects of pre-planning for web searching. The PLUS model's first stage is 'Purpose', which can be used to encourage students to think about their information need before using a search engine. When students use a search engine to find information, it is normally part of a wider need for information, such as an assignment, and it is important that students identify the purpose of the wider need before focusing on searching for specific information. Figure 6.1 shows an example from Ripon Grammar School, UK, of guidance provided to students for identifying a clear purpose. Students complete this form and discuss it with the teacher, before they start planning their web searches.

Many schools now use concept mapping as a means to encourage students to think about their information needs and topic before searching for information. Novak and Canas (2008) provide an excellent guide to concept mapping and their ideas can be translated into practice by teachers and teacher librarians. Recent research by this author showed that students valued concept mapping as a key tool when planning assignments and a precursor to web searching. A typical comment from a year 7 student was 'Your mind map [concept map] helps you to know what you want to find out – and after you've done some searching, you can go back to the map and change it.' Students in this study also favoured formulating questions as a useful planning tool. Figure 6.2 from Springfield High School gives an example of scaffolding, which can be used to help students form questions.

Using effective search strategies

Chapter 2 emphasized the need for teachers and teacher librarians to be effective searchers on the web. It is even more important for students in upper primary, elementary, secondary and high schools to have an effective

---

PLANNING my work

NAME _____ FORM _____

My topic is _____
My research is for what purpose? (What do you need to produce from the information you find?)

My work must include: (How much information do you need? In what format? Do you need pictures, etc.?)

My final written work will be written for what audience? (At what level will you need your information?)

How much time do I have to do this work?
        My research must be completed by _____.

New skills you will learn in this work:
- ✓ how to carefully plan an independent research project (developing questions and keywords, dividing and managing work)
- ✓ how to select the best resources to use (using selection criteria, skimming and scanning)
- ✓ how to record new information, analysing it and synthesizing it into your existing knowledge
- ✓ how to form conclusions and back those up with reasons and evidence to prove your claims
- ✓ how to monitor and self-evaluate your work and make changes when necessary
- ✓ how to collaborate with others to work together toward a common goal.

Figure 6.1 Student scaffold for identifying purpose at Ripon Grammar School, UK

search strategy. Research by Bilal, Sarangthem and Bachir (2008) and Chung and Neuman (2007), among others, has shown that students generally lack effective search strategies, and need guidance on how to search the web.

One of the key differences between staff and students when creating search strategies is that students are likely to need an explanation of why they need a search strategy. This is crucial as most students think that web searching is easy. Thus there needs to be a preliminary discussion with students about what a search strategy is before explaining how to construct one. A way to achieve this is to brainstorm the term 'search strategy' with students, asking them for possible alternatives. Students are likely to come up with terms such as 'search plan' or 'search path', but the key benefit is to encourage students to think about why they need to be effective searchers. This can also be done by splitting students into groups, and asking each one to produce a concept map on 'How to be a good web searcher'. The groups

Question Brainstormer

	Topic #1	Topic # 2
Which one? (Collect information to make an informed choice.) Eg. Which 20th Century president did the most to promote civil rights?		
How? (Understand problems and perspectives,weigh options, and propose solutions.) Eg. How should we solve the problem of water pollution in our neighborhood?		
What if? (Use the knowledge you have to pose a hypothesis and consider options.) Eg. What if the Declaration of Independence abolished slavery?		
Should? (Make a moral or practical decision based on evidence.) Eg. Should we clone humans?		
Why? (Understand and explain relationships to get to the essence of a complicated issue.) Eg. Why do people abuse children?		

Brainstorm two topics related to the unit we are studying. Use the cues to develop essential questions that will help you focus your research. You don't need to fill in every box. We will be discussing which of the questions you develop would be the best to research.

Back to Virtual Library

Figure 6.2 Guidance on forming questions from Springfield Township High School, USA (www.sdst.org/shs/library/questbrain.html)

can then compare the concept maps and in this way students learn about searching from each other.

Figure 6.3 is part of a presentation on effective searching from Dixie Grammar School. The presentation, which uses the Prezi (http://prezie.com) tool, zooms in on key aspects of searching such as 'Do you think about your search terms?'.

Figure 6.4. is an example of advice given to students at Springfield Township High School on searching. This type of advice, contained in many school library websites, will be much more meaningful to students who have been encouraged to reflect on why they need a search strategy, such as in the brainstorming example given above.

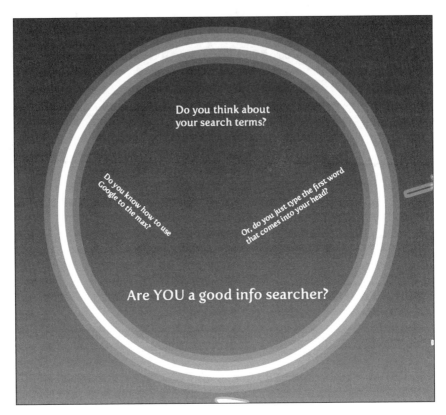

Figure 6.3 Guidance for students at the Dixie Grammar School, UK, on searching (http://library-online.org.uk/2010/06/welcome-to-sixth-form-historians)

How to structure a good search engine query:
- Brainstorm several key words and phrases, the ones you think would appear in your dream document.
- Also consider the words that should NOT appear in your dream documents, for instance when researching the planet Saturn, you'll want to eliminate references to cars and automobiles. With Dolphins, you'll likely want to avoid football.
- Understand syntax, or the language of the search engine. This is revealed in the help or tips page and will guide you to how to use that tool most effectively.
- Put most important words and phrases first.
- Search nouns first.
- Consider phrases in which words are likely to appear next to each other in exact order, for example names like '?Martin Luther King?' Or '?vitamin A?'.
- Focus on nouns (verbs are often vague; stop words like articles 'a', 'an' and 'the' are ignored by most engines).

Figure 6.4 Advice on searching from Springfield Township High School

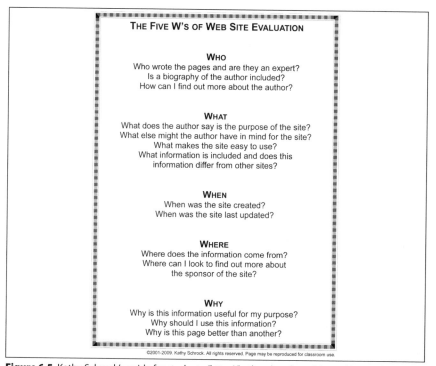

THE FIVE W'S OF WEB SITE EVALUATION

WHO
Who wrote the pages and are they an expert?
Is a biography of the author included?
How can I find out more about the author?

WHAT
What does the author say is the purpose of the site?
What else might the author have in mind for the site?
What makes the site easy to use?
What information is included and does this
information differ from other sites?

WHEN
When was the site created?
When was the site last updated?

WHERE
Where does the information come from?
Where can I look to find out more about
the sponsor of the site?

WHY
Why is this information useful for my purpose?
Why should I use this information?
Why is this page better than another?

Figure 6.5 Kathy Schrock's guide for students (http://kathyschrock.net/abceval/5ws.pdf)

Evaluating websites and web-based information

As with effective searching, website evaluation is a challenging task for many students. Although there are many guides for website evaluation, such as Kathy Schrock's guide shown in Figure 6.5, not all guides found on the web are suitable for school students, as many are written for university students and the terminology may be too difficult. Teaching students how to evaluate websites should include explaining the value of evaluating sites and how to complete this evaluation. A session similar to that for effective searching, where students in groups are asked to produce a concept map or guide of the benefits of website evaluation, and then to share their ideas with other groups, can be an excellent starting point for students. If students are able to reflect on why they should evaluate the websites they find, they are much more likely to use the guides provided by teachers and teacher librarians. Figure 6.6 shows a guide for students at Hutchinson High School; this sort of guide can be used as a discussion item for students, to help them construct their own guides in the language used by

---

Web page evaluation

These questions will help you to evaluate the information on the internet sites you find when doing research. Remember to evaluate the sites according to these six topics to make sure that the research you find is what you want and need.

Relevancy:

Did I use keywords and questions relevant to my search?

Is the information relevant to my topic?

Appropriateness:

Is the information suitable for my age and core values?

Will the information help me answer my research question?

Details:

How much information do I need?

Is the depth of the coverage of the topic adequate for my needs?

Currency:

When was the information published or last updated?

Is the information old and outdated?

Authority:

Who is the author of the information?

What are his or her qualifications?

Bias:

Why was this information written?

Was the site written to inform me, persuade me, or sell me something?

Figure 6.6 Guide for students at Hutchinson High School, USA (www.usd308.com/hhslibrary/webpage_evaluation.htm); RADCAB developed by Highsmith, Inc., 2007

the class. This approach is also likely to give more ownership of any guide to the students.

Reading for information

Once students have found a website and used their website evaluation criteria to judge its suitability, their key task is to read, interpret and use the information and ideas that they find on the website. Reading for information requires students to use a range of skills, including searching for information on the site by using keywords, skimming and scanning; identifying key sections of the website in text, graphic or video format; interpreting what they find in relation to their purpose; and taking notes on what they find.

The complexity of *reading* a website, as opposed to *using* a website is often misunderstood, and too often teachers and teacher librarians make assumptions about students' abilities – they assume that students will have been taught how to read and interpret information found on websites at an earlier stage of their education. This author's research shows that such assumptions are false. Information literacy sessions taught by teachers and teacher librarians often do not focus in any depth on reading for information. Students need to have the opportunity to identify these skills for themselves, for example, in brainstorming sessions with teachers or teacher librarians. At Dunbar Grammar School in the UK, the English teacher working with year 8 students includes a lesson on reading for information for his students who are completing an essay on a topical area of their choice, such as climate change. The brainstorming session, in which students make suggestions which are discussed and recorded when most students agree, includes:

- how to find different points of view on the web
- how to distinguish between opinion and evidence on the web
- how to establish the authority of the author on the website
- how to verify evidence found on the web
- how to decide the relevance of information found on the web
- what to do if you have difficulty in understanding the content of a website.

The value of the students themselves discussing aspects of web use such as these is that they are more likely to put what they learned in the classroom into practice. The students argued that this was more valuable than being directed to a guide for using the web effectively.

Reflecting on web use

In all the information literacy models referred to in this book there is an element of teaching students to reflect on what they have achieved in their learning or when they have completed an assignment. In the PLUS model, the self-evaluation stage includes asking students to reflect on how effectively they found and used information, and on their use of the web. Whether teachers and teacher librarians use an information literacy model or not, key questions which can be posed for students include:

◆ How well did you plan your search?
◆ Did you use your mind map to help you search for the right information?
◆ Did you use your questions to help you find the right information?
◆ Did you use the advanced search as well as the search option?
◆ How did you decide whether a website was useful or not?
◆ How did you look for information within the websites you found?
◆ Did you need to go back and revise your search keywords?
◆ What did you learn about searching the web for information?

Teachers and teacher librarians can incorporate versions of these questions into student assignments, by requiring students to provide answers to the questions as an integral part of preparing an assignment. In this way, students become accustomed to viewing reflection on their searching as a normal part of completing an assignment, not as an add-on which is separate from the assignment itself. In Ripon Grammar School, UK, students are asked to set themselves goals before starting an assignment, one of which relates to improving the way students search the web (see Figure 6.7).

Using information resources effectively, part 1: taking notes

From the resources you have evaluated, choose the best three to start; use the others only if you have time.

For each resource:

- Quickly skim over the pages you identified as being useful (like the polar bear on ice skates!).
- *Stay focused* on your questions while you *scan* over the text to find the part you need to read (like the polar bear looking for salmon with a magnifying glass!).
- Read the selected text carefully all the way through.
- Put what you have just read into your own words in your head.
- Take out all the unnecessary words (remember our Humpty Dumpty exercise!), then write down the ten words that represent the most important ideas from what you have read.

The important thing about recording ideas is that it is not copying! Read the text, think about what you have read and only copy down NUTS:

- something *new* to you
- something *useful* to your purpose
- something you can *tell* to *someone* else (your own words . . . and as few as are absolutely necessary!).

Figure 6.7 Guide to reading for information using the PLUS model at Ripon Grammar School, UK

Developing a personal model for web use

Although teachers and teacher librarians have successfully used information literacy models, such as the PLUS, Big 6, ISP and NSW DET models (or adapted versions of these models), it can be argued that an attempt should be made to allow students to develop their own models of information literacy rather than have them imposed on them. These would be more likely to suit their learning style. Most students in upper primary, elementary, secondary or high schools are able to reflect on how they use a range of information literacy skills, including use of the web. In some schools visited by this author, students are encouraged to reflect in groups on how they plan for searching the web and how they carry out searches, but this tends to be a one-off exercise. Having carried out such sessions, teachers and teacher librarians often assume that students will follow the advice of their peers or school staff in their future use of the web. In reality, students often quickly forget what they discuss in these sessions and return to old habits.

If students could be asked to draw up their own, individual guide to using the web and to develop it as they progress through their school years, students' use of the web could improve dramatically. There is an expectation that students will reflect on their web use and become more effective web users as they grow older and more experienced. Most research, including this author's research on transfer (Herring, 2010), shows that most students do not transfer skills and abilities in web use across subject or time. If students had a personal model which they carried with them, and, importantly, which teachers and teacher librarians encouraged them to use and develop, students would own the model and would perhaps be more motivated to be reflective practitioners. There appears to be no research on personal information literacy models or personal web use models, but projects in schools relating to personal models could seek to:

- develop versions of personal models with upper primary, elementary or lower high school students, for example using concept maps or flow charts or other graphical tools
- conduct sessions where students compared and contrasted individual models and formed their own terminology for their models
- develop a school wide plan for reinforcing use of personal plans across the curriculum when students were involved in information seeking and use on the web, for example requiring students to use their personal

model in assignments and reflect on the use of the personal model
◆ share the findings of the project with other schools and other teachers and teacher librarians.

It is likely that each teacher and teacher librarian in a school has their own personal model of web use, although this may never have been explored mentally or put into text or graphic form. A useful prerequisite to students developing personal information literacy or web use models would be for teachers and teacher librarians to develop them, perhaps in an in-service session.

Conclusion

The development of students as web learners rather than web users is a major challenge for schools, and teachers and teacher librarians face a challenge in convincing all school staff that the skills and abilities involved in effective web use should be taught and reinforced across the curriculum and not just in the school library. The benefits from developing students as effective web learners are that students can relate web use to their own learning styles, and use the web thoughtfully and not mechanically. If students can be convinced that each web search is a new challenge and potentially a new learning experience, then their web use, and in turn their learning, will improve.

References

Bilal, D., Sarangthem, S. and Bachir, I. (2008) Toward a Model of Children's Information Seeking Behavior in Using Digital Libraries. In *Proceedings of the Second International Symposium on Information Interaction in Context*, ACM, 145–51.

Chung, J. and Neuman, D. (2007) High School Students' Information Seeking and Use for Class Projects, *Journal of the American Society for Information Science and Technology*, **58** (10), 1503–17.

Herring, J. (2010) *School Students, Question Formulation and Issues of Transfer: a constructivist grounded analysis*, Libri, in press.

Kuiper, E., Volman, M. and Terwel, J. (2008) Students' Use of Web Literacy Skills and Strategies: searching, reading and evaluating web information, *Information*

Research, **13** (3),
http://informationr.net/ir/13-3/paper351.html.

Novak, J. and Canas, A. (2008) *The Theory Underlying Concept Maps and How to Construct and Use Them,* Institute for Human and Machine Cognition.

Developing learning websites for student use – design and tools

Having read this chapter you will be able to:

- reflect on the use of learning websites in schools
- evaluate the benefits of designing a learning website for your school
- develop a plan for an effective learning website
- evaluate and use a range of learning website design tools
- develop an in-service course on website design for your school staff.

Introduction

This chapter focuses on teachers and teacher librarians as the creators of customized learning websites in school. There is a plethora of information on the web relating to the subjects being taught in schools. There are also examples of learning websites designed by other teachers and teacher librarians on the web. Although these sources can be useful, they often have to be adapted and are not designed to meet the needs of a particular group of students in a particular school. The advent of easy to use tools now makes it much easier and quicker for teachers and teacher librarians to design their own learning websites, which can be designed to be much more relevant and personal to students. For example, a learning website designed by a geography teacher and a teacher librarian which states that it was designed for year 8 students in School X studying climate change, and which includes the opportunity for student input, is much more likely to be seen as valuable by students than a general website.

The aim of this chapter is to provide teachers and teacher librarians with examples of tools that can be used to design learning websites of a particular kind, providing students with a package that contains elements of what they are studying, the assignment to be completed, mediated resources related to the topic being studied, and information literacy advice on learning from these resources and about completing the assignment. This approach is different from one that provides students merely with a list of websites related to their topic. The focus of this chapter is on designing such sites and learning to use a range of tools. Chapter 9 will focus on the content of learning websites and discuss examples of content.

This chapter provides this author's definition of learning websites and the benefits derived from developing such sites, evaluates approaches to website design, examines a range of tools for developing learning websites, and offers an example of an in-service session on developing learning websites.

Learning websites

This author defines learning websites as websites developed in a particular school, for a particular group of students who are studying a curricular topic. They may also be termed local learning websites as, although they may be adapted for use in other schools, they are focused on the needs of a local group of students. A learning website is designed so that students are involved not just in using the site to access to digital resources, but also in learning when using the site. This learning may relate to a subject or may take the form of reinforcing information literacy skills and abilities. Student engagement is also an integral part of a learning website, as is the inclusion of text, graphics and possibly video. As a learning website is designed for students in their own school, ownership of the site by students, teachers and teacher librarians is an important aspect of a learning website.

Learning websites are also referred to as instructional websites (Herring, 2004) although that term tends to focus on teaching rather than learning. Another term for learning websites is 'learning objects', which is used to cover a wide range of educational websites designed to meet the needs of the school curriculum. The key aspects of learning objects, according to Lowe et al. (2010), should include presenting a challenge to students, motivating students to learn, having a clear learning purpose, and including quality and graphics. Teachers and teacher librarians have access to collections of learning object in different countries, for example The Le@rning Federation (www.thelearningfederation.edu.au) in Australia. Although these learning objects are very useful resources and of very high quality, they are often commercially produced and try to cater generally for students studying curricular topics. They are not designed for local use and it may be harder to engage students in externally produced learning objects. Thus in-school produced learning websites, if well designed, are likely to engage students more than some learning objects.

Website design

Developing a website used to be a very technical process, in which the teacher or teacher librarian had to learn how to use HTML and had to edit the computer code in the site. Nowadays website packages such as Wikispaces (www.wikispaces.com) or Yola (www.yola.com) do not require users to use HTML. The technical side of website development is much easier than in the past, but the design elements remain very important. There are many guides to websites design on the web for teachers and teacher librarians; Pappas' (2000) guide remains an excellent starting point for designing a learning website. This recommends that developing a website should include:

- ◆ brainstorming – thinking about possible content for the website
- ◆ developing and revising categories of the main content (see Figure 7.1)
- ◆ making a flowchart to show how pages on the site will link to each other
- ◆ developing a plan of how users will navigate the site, for example how users can always return to the home page from anywhere on the site
- ◆ considering the layout of pages, ensuring that the design across the website is consistent.

The first element of designing a learning website should be to identify its purpose and this can be done by asking various questions, such as: Why is this website being developed? The answers should include a statement on how the website will enhance the teaching of a subject, for example earthquakes, and provide an e-resource which students can use inside and outside school. A second question might be: Who is this website for? The answers should demonstrate that the website will meet the needs of a particular group of students, for example those in year 7 who are studying the causes and effects of earthquakes. This might be broken down further

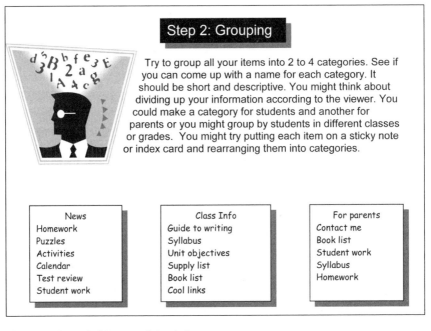

Figure 7.1 Pappas' advice on website design
(www.edteck.com/eddesign/web_docs/Bottom_up.pdf)

by identifying groups within year 7 classes such as students with reading difficulties, students whose first language is not English, and gifted and talented students. A third question might be: What is this website trying to achieve? The answers should show how the website will help improve students' use of resources, such as reading for information about earthquakes and evaluating the content of websites.

One of the best sources for designing websites is Lynch and Horton's *Web Style Guide* (2008), which emphasizes the importance of identifying a clear purpose for the website, arguing, 'A short statement identifying two or three goals should be the foundation of your web site design.'

A second stage in website design is the development of a story board for the site. Smith (2006) provides a short but instructive guide to designing a story board, which is a plan for the site which is developed on paper, before using a web design package. An excellent way of designing a story board for a learning website, and one used by this author with teachers and teacher librarians, is to use a large sheet of paper and Post-it notes. Before using the large paper, an A4 sheet can be used to draw up an outline plan of the website. Figure 7.2. shows an example of part of an outline plan. The use of Post-it notes means that discussions can take place on the larger

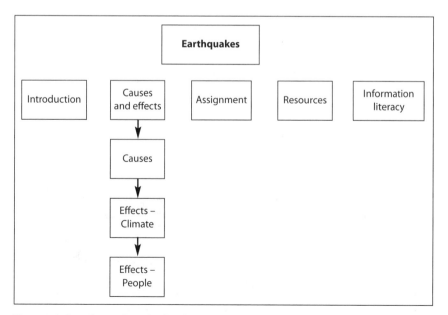

Figure 7.2 Part of an outline plan for a learning website

paper and the notes can be moved around. Figure 7.3 shows an example of a story board.

Once the website has been planned, there are a number of key aspects of design which need to be taken into consideration. Pappas (2000), Lynch and Horton (2008) and other web design experts stress the following points as important:

◆ *Format* – The users of the website will expect there to be a consistent format within the site. For example, navigation icons that lead the users to other pages or back to the home page should always be in the same place. Where the site has a sidebar, giving the contents of the site, this should appear on all pages. Consistency of format is a key feature of a successful site.

◆ *Template* – Most website design packages offer the web developer a range of templates which can be used. When developing a learning

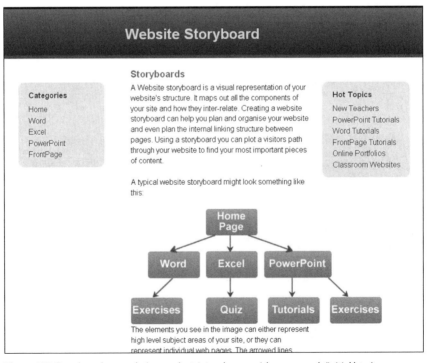

Figure 7.3 Storyboard example (www.electricteacher.com/classroomweb/initial.htm); reproduced with permission of Microsoft.com

website, a suitable template needs to be chosen – one that is attractive to students but not garish, or one that will lead the students to regard the site as providing entertainment.

◆ *Colour* – The choice of colours used on a site will have an impact on the site's usability. Teachers and teacher librarians should avoid colours that are very bright, and it is often wise to start with a conservative approach to colour, for example to use mainly black text. The use of different colours should be an aid to the user, but colours should not be used to try to impress students.

◆ *Navigation* – The ability of all users, including those with sight problems, to move smoothly around and outside the site is very important. Where users are led to outside links, the developers should ensure that the external website opens in a new tab or new window.

◆ *Links* – In a learning website, there will be a resources section, which leads students to external websites. Teachers and teacher librarians should ensure that these links are to specific parts of websites, taking students to the exact location they need. For example a link on 'earthquakes' might lead students to a specific part of the US Geological Society that focuses on earthquakes, and not to the Society's home page. Links should not force the students to navigate an external site. Links also need to be regularly checked; there are a number of tools on the web which will check for broken links, including Xenu's Link Sleuth (http://home.snafu.de/tilman/xenulink.html).

◆ *Accessibility* – Learning websites should cater, as far as possible, for all students, including those with disabilities. Teachers and teacher librarians should check disability organizations, such as national sight impairment societies, to ensure that students with sight problems can either read all the site's content easily, or are provided with alternatives.

◆ *Graphics, sound and video* – Although the use of graphics, sound and video on a learning website can enhance the site, for example where a podcast advising students about completing an assignment is included, such features can also be seen as unnecessary and self-indulgent additions. Students are used to accessing sophisticated music and video sites, so teachers and teacher librarians should ensure that any graphics, sound and video are of high quality and use copyright free photographs. Student produced material in graphical, sound or video format is likely to enhance the site.

These points do not constitute an exhaustive list but are key elements in producing usable and attractive learning websites. If they are taken into account, the website will prove to be an effective learning resource for students.

Website development tools

One of the key developments on the web in the last five years has been the growth of Web 2.0 (see Chapter 4), and there has been an expansion in the number of website design tools available to teachers and teacher librarians. The tools discussed here are examples of some of the most common packages used in schools across the world. These are not definitive examples and new tools are constantly appearing. Keeping up to date with new tools for developing learning resources is an important aspect of continuing professional development for teachers and teacher librarians. The tools evaluated here are for the development of wikis, websites and presentations.

Wikis

The use of wikis in schools has become relatively common in a short space of time. A wiki is a website which allows a range of users to add content. The most well known wiki is Wikipedia (http://en.wikipedia.org), which has developed into one of the most used encyclopaedias on the web. TeachersFirst (2010) provides a useful starting guide to using wikis in schools and suggests that a wiki might be used 'as the organizational and intellectual epicenter of your class – Wiki all assignments, projects, collaboration, rubrics, etc.'; for collaborative projects carried out by student groups or by school staff; as a collection of resources on a particular topic; a report, including photographs and video, of a field trip; and as a revision tool for students.

Wikispaces (www.wikispaces.com/site/for/teachers) is an educational wiki creation package. Like all wiki tools, Wikispaces requires the website developer to register in order to set up a new wiki. Once registered, the developer chooses a title for the wiki, which then acquires a discrete URL; for example http://earlyconvictlife.wikispaces.com was created by one of this author's students. A wiki creator can choose for their wiki to be public – anyone can add or edit content, protected – anyone can view the wiki but only members can edit it, or private – only members can view or edit the content. For teachers and teacher librarians in schools, the protected option is useful, as it allows students and staff outside the school to view the content, in the spirit of sharing, but does not allow anyone other than staff or students to edit the content. This protection is important where students are uploading content to the wiki and can be a reassurance to parents.

Wikis have a very simple feature, which enables the novice to input content into a blank page and then save that page. New pages can be created and edited, and text, graphics, sound and video can be added. Figure 7.4 shows the home page for students studying climate change at Tourtellotte Memorial High School, USA. The page shows that the site is protected and there are links to other pages in the sidebar on the left, in this case to class teams studying aspects of climate change. Figure 7.5 shows material created by Team 1, which uses graphics well and allows other students to click on the topics such as 'Our position', in which the student team gives its opinion on the debate.

Other packages of similar value to teachers and teacher librarians include PBWorks (https://my.pbworks.com) and Wetpaint (www.wetpaint.com).

Figure 7.4 Home page on climate change by Tourtellotte Memorial High School, USA (http://climatechangedebate.wikispaces.com)

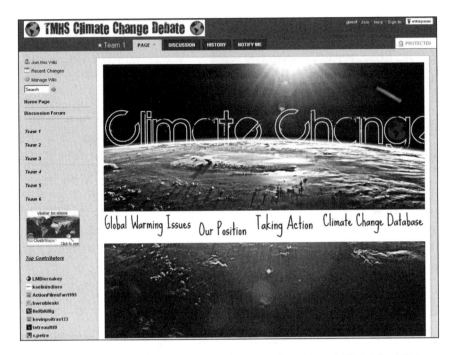

Figure 7.5 The Team 1 page on climate change from Tourtellotte Memorial High School, USA (http://climatechangedebate.wikispaces.com/Team+1)

Teachers and teacher librarians should sample different wiki creation packages before deciding which to use.

Websites

Wiki tools come in a particular format, which can be seen as restrictive if learning website developers wish to have more freedom in the design of their website. New website creation packages such as Webs (www.webs.com), Weebly (www.weebly.com) and Yola (www.yola.com) have a number of common features. One of the most flexible aspects of website development tools is that they offer teachers and teacher librarians a range of templates. For example Webs offers over 300 different templates, a sample of which can be seen in Figure 7.6. Most packages offer the facility of changing the template at a later stage.

Another feature of web development tools is that teachers and teacher librarians can add and edit content very easily, so that text (for example an

Figure 7.6 Templates offered by Webs when registering for a new website
(http://members.webs.com/s/signup?execution=e2s1)

explanation of parameters about climate change), graphics (for example photographs of the effects of climate change from Flickr's Creative Commons), sound (for example a podcast on climate change by the teacher or external expert) and video (for example a link to a video presenting different views on climate change) can be integrated into the site.

Other aspects include blogs and/or forums for student discussion or input to class activities. Weebly and Webs offer users the opportunity to include a blog on the site, and Weebly states that its blogs come 'with full comment moderation features allowing an open, moderated, or closed conversation'. Most packages also offer a mechanism to protect the site by requiring visitors to sign on with a user name and password; as with wikis discussed above, this can provide protection and allow students' work to be displayed with reasonable assurance that it will be protected.

One advantage that Weebly has over other packages is that it guarantees that no advertising will appear on the site. For younger students, this is certainly a bonus and it may be for older students also, although they may be less likely to be distracted by advertising.

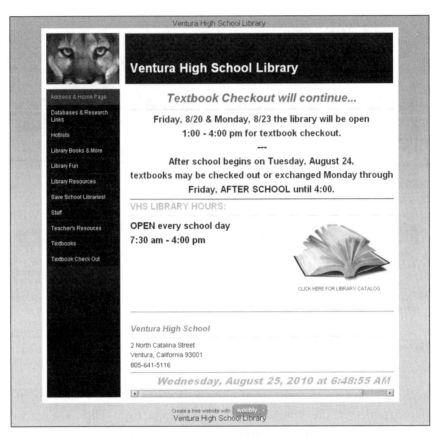

Figure 7.7 Ventura High School Library, USA (http://vhslibrary.weebly.com

Perhaps the key feature of these website development packages is that they are free and teachers and teacher librarians can set up sophisticated websites without having to pay. All the packages have add-ons for which the user must pay, including buying a domain, for example having vhslibrary.com instead of vhslibrary.weebly.com.

Figure 7.7 shows an example of a Weebly site and Figure 7.8 shows a site developed using Webs.

There are thus many advantages for teachers and teacher librarians to set up their learning websites using packages such as Webs or Weebly. It is important that school staff keep backups of material on their websites as there is no guarantee that the companies that host their sites will remain in business for ever. As new and more flexible packages are likely to appear in the next five years, teachers and teacher librarians should be prepared to

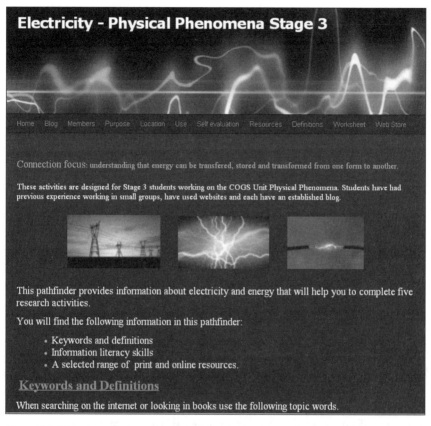

Figure 7.8 A learning website on electricity for students at Forestville Public School (www.carolynfarrugia.webs.com)

consider changing their website host, if this would lead to considerable educational benefits.

Presentations

Although there have been new developments in packages, which allow teachers and teacher librarians to deliver presentations to their students, these tools have been limited. For example, PowerPoint is a widely used tool in schools, but it tends to be a static form of presentation, although it can include graphics and links to video clips. More recent packages have offered school staff and students the opportunity to create presentations which can be hosted on a wiki or website more easily. Two of the most commented on

Figure 7.9 Animoto presentation by Andrew Marcinek
(www.classroom20.com/forum/topics/hello-animoto)

and most often used in schools are Animoto (http://animoto.com) and Prezi (www.prezi.com).

Animoto is a video-making tool, which can be used by teachers, teacher librarians and students. Marcinek (2009) argues that Animoto is very simple to use and far less complicated than standard video-editing packages. Marcinek states that he has 'used Animoto for back to school nights and in my Language Arts classes to help students understand themes, characterization and symbolism within the novels we cover'. The tool is free to schools and teachers and teacher librarians can use a standard video recorder to make a short film. Animoto can then be used to show excerpts from the film and set them to music.

Figure 7.9 shows the title page of an Animoto presentation by Marcinek (2009). Other examples of using Animoto are in an introduction to the library (Durst, 2009), in a science class, on a field trip and in a library video from Rockingham County Public Schools, USA (RCPS, 2010).

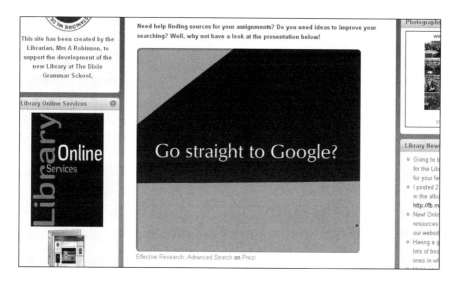

Figure 7.10 Encouraging students to reflect on research at The Dixie Grammar School, UK (http://library-online.org.uk/2010/06/welcome-to-sixth-form-historians)

Prezi allows users to present images, rather than video, to engage students in a topic. The key feature is the zoom, which allows the teacher or teacher librarian to zoom in on part of an image in order to emphasize a particular point (for example the importance of a valve in the body) or to provide a picture or a definition (for example of a type of insect). Hill (2010) argues that if they use Prezi carefully, teachers can engage students when explaining curricular topics, but advises that the zoom feature needs to be used with care. Hill gives examples of Prezi being used for in-service training with teachers and as a support to teaching science at St Mary Redcliffe and Temple School, UK. Robinson (2010) used Prezi as part of information literacy guidance for her year 12 students and to view the tool as an alternative way of engaging students and encouraging them to think about using information literacy skills. Figure 7.10 shows an image from the information literacy presentation, asking students to reflect on the question: What is research?

Animoto and Prezi are examples of presentation tools that can potentially be used by teachers and teacher librarians. Cool Tools for Schools (2010) presents a list of 24 presentation packages that can be used for staff and students. Teachers and teacher librarians can select the tools that suit their circumstances, for example the amount of time available to learn new tools, and use them for teaching and learning.

In-service training on website design

As there are many pressures on school staff to use ICT in the classroom and school library, and many teachers and teacher librarians often view new software tools as potentially extremely time-consuming, it is often difficult to persuade school staff to try out new approaches. Teachers and teacher librarians often view themselves more as *users* of learning resources than *creators*. Providing in-service training can allow school staff to work together and allay some of the fears which might exist.

Figure 7.11 shows an in-service session run by this author with teachers and teacher librarians in Australia and the UK. The emphasis in this session is on collaborative working so that individual staff do not feel that website design should be an isolated task.

Storyboarding a learning website

Aims
- to review storyboarding techniques for the development of learning websites
- to provide library teams with an opportunity to practice storyboarding for a learning website.

Method
1. In sub-groups of five, library team members will design the structure of a learning website using the storyboard technique. A useful guide to storyboarding can be seen at **www.wtvi.com/html/handout.html** – see attached page for the advice given. You might also consult the web style guide at **http://webstyleguide.com/wsg3/1-process/7-development-process.html**, which argues that as web designers you need to:

    - decide on the goals of your site
    - decide on the audience
    - decide on content.

2. The focus of this exercise will be on developing a site to teach students how to read a website when researching volcanoes.
3. Each sub-group should try to create a well planned, attractive and easy to use learning website. Think of labels or phrases to describe your goals, your audience and your content, and write down each label on a sticky note. Then try to group them in some order. Websites are established on some sort of hierarchy, so decide your top level of information. Think of what will go on your home page. Think of navigational paths – how users will seek out the information they require. You can experiment using the labels provided and arranging them onto a large sheet of paper. There is no right or wrong way and it may take several attempts and modifications before a final decision can be made.
4. Each sub-group will post their design on the wall and we will discuss aspects of design for learning websites.

Figure 7.11 In-service training session on website design

Conclusion

This chapter has focused on learning websites and how teachers and teacher librarians can become creators of tailor made learning resources for their students. It has emphasised the importance of creating a view of what a learning website might include for a particular school or subject within that school. There has also been a focus on the skills and tools needed to create learning websites.

This author takes the view that the ideas and tools presented here are now a normal part of working life for teachers and teacher librarians, and that using the approaches and tools discussed here can make a real contribution to learning and teaching in the school. If the teacher or teacher librarian can be seen as a creator of learning resources, then there is a greater possibility of students also becoming resource creators and taking a more active part in their learning. ICT now provides tools which are much simpler than those of even five years ago, and provide teachers and teacher librarians with opportunities to become more involved in designing and delivering locally produced learning resources for their students.

References

Durst, J. (2009) *Penleigh and Essendon Grammar School: Animoto*, http://slav.globalteacher.org.au/picture-gallery/penleigh-and-essendon-grammar-school-animoto.

Herring, J. (2004) *The Internet and Information Skills: a guide for teachers and school librarians*, Facet Publishing.

Hill, P. (2010) *Thoughts on Using Prezi as a Teaching Tool*, http://prezi.com/rfsnedhqmhqa/thoughts-on-using-prezi-as-a-teaching-tool.

Lowe, K, Lee, L., Schibeci, R., Cummings, R., Phillips, R. and Lake, D. (2010) Learning Objects and Engagement of Students in Australian and New Zealand Schools, *British Journal of Educational Technology*, **41** (2), 227–41.

Lynch, P and Horton, S. (2008) *Web Style Guide: basic design principles for designing websites*, 3rd edn, Yale University Press, www.webstyleguide.com/wsg3/index.html.

Marcinek, A. (2009) *Hello Animoto*, Classroom 2.0, www.classroom20.com/forum/topics/hello-animoto.

Pappas, P. (2000) *Design Your Website From the Bottom Up*, www.edteck.com/eddesign/web_docs/Bottom_up.pdf.

Robinson, A. (2010) *Effective Research: advanced search*,
    http://library-online.org.uk/2010/06/welcome-to-sixth-form-historians.
Rockingham County Public Schools (2010) *Using Animoto in RCPS*,
    www.rockingham.k12.va.us/screencasts/animoto/animoto.htm.
Smith, W. (2006) *How to Storyboard Your Website*,
    http://e-articles.info/e/a/title/How-to-Storyboard-Your-Web-Site.
TeachersFirst (2010),
    www.teachersfirst.com/content/wiki/wikiideas1.cfm.

Developing learning websites for student use – content

Having read this chapter you will be able to:

- plan and develop content for a learning website
- develop curricular content for a learning website
- develop e-pathfinders for your students
- incorporate information literacy guidance for students in learning websites
- develop learning websites which encourage student participation.

Introduction

As was emphasized in Chapter 7, learning resources for students that are focused on the needs of particular groups of students studying curricular topics in schools are more likely to be seen by students as being designed specifically for them rather than for any students in general. Locally produced learning websites will motivate students more than general ones as the students will recognize not only the name of the school and their class on the website, but also the direct link between what they are learning in the classroom, or what assignment they are completing, and the content of the website. If students can be involved in the further development of a learning website, for example by adding web sources which they have found and evaluated, then this is also likely to motivate and engage students.

Deciding on the content of learning websites can be a challenge for teachers and teacher librarians. The content of learning websites needs to be guided by the needs of the student group for which the site is designed. Chapter 7 examined aspects of good design for learning websites, but a well designed site with content that does not match the needs of students, for example has an inappropriate level of language, will not be successful. In deciding on content, teachers and teacher librarians also need to consider differentiation, as student groups are likely to include a range of abilities and reading levels, particularly at the primary or elementary level and early secondary or high school level.

This chapter will focus on presenting subject content in learning websites, developing e-pathfinders, and enhancing student participation in wikis and blogs. The aim is to present a range of ideas for developing the content of learning websites and to provide examples which can be adapted by teachers and teacher librarians for their own schools.

Subject content

Including subject content in a learning website can give students an experience of online learning, which can be beneficial for students as online learning is likely to increase in the future. Teachers and teacher librarians planning a learning website have to decide what to include in the subject content part of the website. For example, if a year 8 group of students is studying development in geography, as in the example from Wycombe High School, UK, in Figure 8.1, a decision needs to be made on the purpose of the

Figure 8.1 Development defined in a geography learning website at Wycombe High School, UK (http://whs.moodledo.co.uk/course/view.php?id=1378)

subject-related material in this section of the website. In this example, first a definition of development is provided, followed by links to PowerPoint presentations and student worksheets. This is a very good example of not crowding the site with too much text.

A learning website should be dynamic and engage the students in activities. If the teacher wants students to read extended passages of text about development, then they can provide a link to a suitable book or website. The subject content of a learning website can be seen as an extension of what is taught in the classroom and an opportunity for students to use the site to complete activities that will extend their learning.

Figure 8.2 shows another example from Wycombe High School, UK, again providing a definition. When students click on the link 'Animated Coasts' they are taken to a web page on animated coasts (Figure 8.3), and can view a series of animations related to coasts. Where students view the learning website as encouraging active participation, rather than reading text, they are more likely to be engaged in the subject and more motivated to be active learners.

Developing e-pathfinders as learning websites

Pathfinders have been used in school, public and academic libraries for many

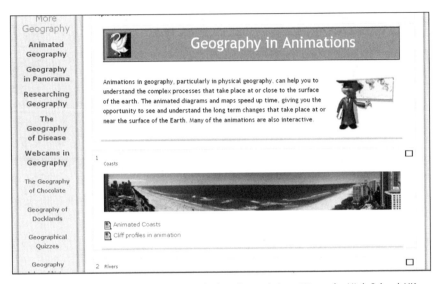

Figure 8.2 Animations defined in a geography learning website at Wycombe High School, UK (http://whs.moodledo.co.uk/course/view.php?id=1365)

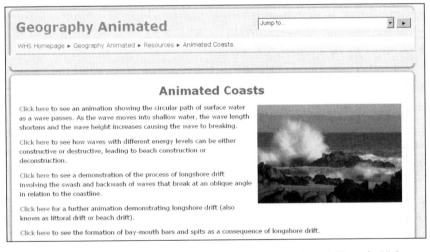

Figure 8.3 Examples of animated coasts in a geography learning website at Wycombe High School, UK (http://whs.moodledo.co.uk/mod/resource/view.php?id=963)

years to provide users with a guide to resources available in the library. In pre-web days, pathfinders were printed lists of books, which students could consult in the school library. Today's pathfinders are likely to be online lists of print and digital resources, which have been mediated by teachers and

Figure 8.4 Pathfinder at the John Newberry Elementary School, USA
(http://nb.wsd.wednet.edu/lmc/pathfinders/american_rev_pathfinder.htm)

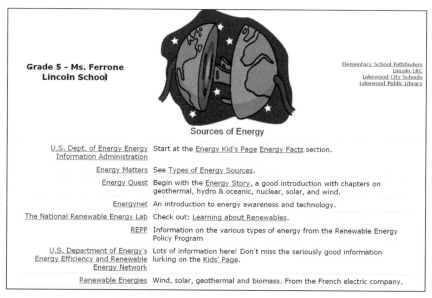

Figure 8.5 Pathfinder at Lincoln School, USA
(www.lkwdpl.org/schools/elempath/energy/index.html)

teacher librarians. Valenza (2010) argues that 'pathfinders lead researchers through information jungles', and the Methuen High School Media Center, USA (2010), states that 'Pathfinders are pages that offer students selected resources in a variety of media on a topic they are researching. They provide a headstart for students as they begin their research project.' Examples of pathfinders can be seen in Figures 8.4 and 8.5. Figure 8.4 shows the front page of a pathfinder from John Newberry Elementary School, USA, and demonstrates the range of information sources – from within and outside the school – which are included in the pathfinder. There is also a guide to keywords, which should be used by students. Figure 8.5 shows a list of resources in a pathfinder from The Lincoln School, USA, and some of the resources are accompanied by short annotations.

Valenza (2010) argues that pathfinders should now take the form of a wiki and provides ten reasons for doing this, including 'Wiki pathfinders allow you to easily upload documents. Your pathfinders can now host your presentations, your handouts, your rubrics, your organizers, as well as models of student work' and 'Wikis are collaborative documents. . . . Wikis allow you to invite individual collaborators (teachers or students or mentors or experts).' This author agrees with Valenza that wikis are an excellent vehicle for pathfinders, but urges teachers and teacher librarians to extend their vision of pathfinders by developing them as learning websites. A pathfinder which is also a learning website should have the following features:

◆ an introduction to a specific audience
◆ keywords and definitions
◆ subject context and content
◆ information literacy guidance
◆ mediated resources accompanied by meaningful annotations.

Introduction

The introduction should provide students with a brief guide to the topic (for example renewable sources), but should also attract students' attention by identifying that this pathfinder has been designed for these students. Figure 8.6 shows the main page of a pathfinder from Burdekin Christian College, Australia, which identifies the audience as students in years 6 and 7. This clearly distinguishes the pathfinder, designed in the school, from general web resources.

The introduction should also state a clear purpose for the pathfinder, for example to increase students' knowledge of renewable sources, and/or to provide support for an assignment on renewable sources. In addition, the

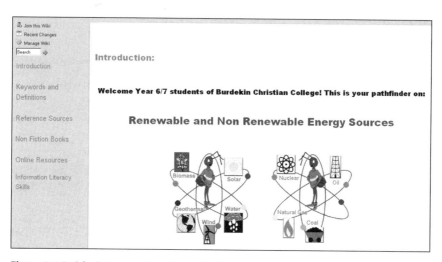

Figure 8.6 Pathfinder introduction at Burdekin Christian College, Australia
(http://librarywikibcc.wikispaces.com)

introduction can explain to students how, having access to sources which have been mediated by the teacher and teacher librarian, they will save time by not having to search for resources. This author has argued that although searching the web is a valuable skill and experience for students, it does not mean that for every topic studied or assignment completed students must be engaged in finding their own resources through web searching.

Keywords and definitions

Providing students with keywords and definitions of key terms within the topic being studied may be seen as spoonfeeding students, but these keywords and definitions are included to help all students think about the parameters and key issues of that topic. The provision of keywords and definitions does not mean that students do not have to develop their own concept map or formulate their own questions. Rather, it provides guidance to students and particularly to less able students.

Figure 8.7 shows an example of a list of keywords and some of the definitions provided to students at Burdekin Christian College, Australia. The keywords listed in the pathfinder can be the results of a brainstorming session, for example on renewable sources, with students in the classroom. The pathfinder thus acts as a reinforcement to what was learned in the

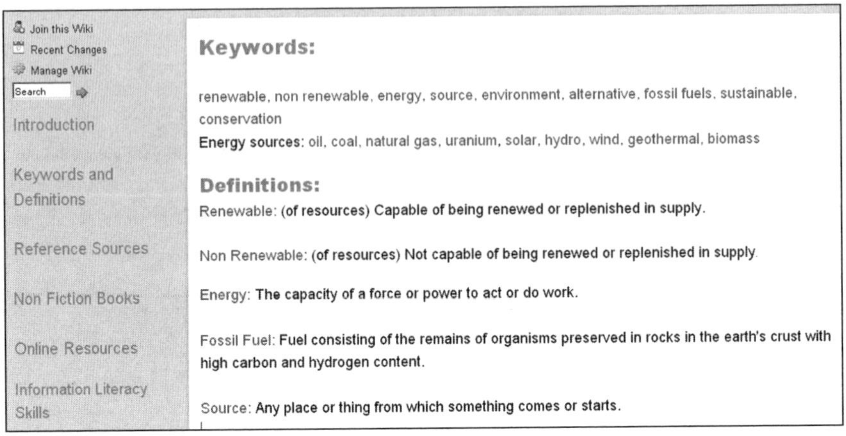

Figure 8.7 Keywords and definitions at Burdekin Christian College, Australia
(http://librarywikibcc.wikispaces.com)

classroom. In some cases, the development of the pathfinder or learning website by a teacher and teacher librarian working collaboratively can encourage the teacher to hold the brainstorming session. Keywords and definitions also encourage students to think about the key aspects of the topic and definitions can be a starting point for students to discover more about a particular aspect of a topic or can suggest at theme for their individual assignment.

Subject context and content

As was discussed above and is demonstrated in Figures 8.1 to 8.3, there is a strong argument for including subject content in a pathfinder which is a learning website, although this is rarely done. The subject content, as with the keywords and definitions, can be a reinforcement tool to remind students of what they learned in the classroom. Subject content can also be given a heading, for example, 'What we learned about renewable sources in class'; then the teacher and teacher librarian can highlight keywords used in the subject content section that also appear in the keywords and definitions section. The inclusion of subject content reminds students that the pathfinder or learning website is an integral part of the subject they are studying, and not an optional add-on.

Purpose:
- What do you already know?
- What do you want to find out?
- What are you going to do with the information?

Location:
- Where can you look to find the right information?
- How can you use the library catalogue to assist you in finding information?
- Can you use the Internet to find relevant information?
- How will you know if the information will be useful?

Use:
- Are you able to skim-read information to find relevant ideas?
- Can you select the right information for your topic?
- Are you able to record the information that you find?
- Are you able to present the information?

Self-Evaluation:
- Have you completed all tasks?
- Have you answered all requirements and questions to the best of your ability?
- How might you improve your research skills in future tasks?

Figure 8.8 The PLUS model reminder for students at Ambarvale Public School, Australia (http://ambarvaleps.pbworks.com)

Information literacy guidance

A key part of any pathfinder that acts as a learning resource for students should be information literacy guidance provided to students. This can take different forms. It may be a reminder to students of the information literacy model used in the school. Figure 8.8 shows a reinforcement of the PLUS model for students at Ambarvale Public School, Australia. Students can be referred to the model in different sections of the pathfinder, as will be seen in the section on annotations below. Guidance can also be more specific and Figure 8.9 from Loreto Kirribilli School, Australia, shows a reflection sheet for students. This is part of the guidance given to students who use the ISP model, and emphasizes the importance of students reflecting on prior knowledge, and on their feelings about defining a topic. The sheet also reminds students that they will be supported by their teachers and teacher librarians. This type of scaffolding for students is effective as it can act as a slowing mechanism for students, some of whom might otherwise rush into searching for information without having defined their purpose.

In pathfinders and learning websites students can be encouraged to develop a concept map for their topic and some school pathfinders provide

HSIE: Modern History, Year 11 Preliminary Course 2010 Historical Investigation - Reflection sheet 1 - SELECTION OF AREA OF INTEREST Due: Term 2, Week 3 - Tuesday 4ᵗʰ May This is the first of four short Reflection sheets you will write during the course of this assignment. Ensure your annotated notetaking grid and bibliography scaffold is up to date on the wiki. Your teacher and the teacher librarians will check on your progress and offer help if you need it. You are NOT expected to have identified the question in your topic yet.
Name
Area of interest
Why are you interested in this area?
What do you already know about your topic?
Have you any particular difficulties relating to your topic? For example, understanding the context of your topic, locating specific resources, feelings of overload or confusion? Please list:

Figure 8.9 Reflection sheet for students at Loreto Kirribilli School, Australia

students with a link to a guide to concept mapping or examples of concept maps. Figure 8.10 shows an example of a concept map provided to students at Lincoln High School, USA, which uses the Big 6 model as a scaffold for students completing assignments. Students can also be given advice on searching the web, once they have adequately defined their topic. This can take the form of a link to a guide developed in the school or elsewhere, for example Internet Tutorials (http://internettutorials.net). Figure 8.11 shows an example of a guide to searching developed by Springfield Township High School, USA.

As with other aspects of information literacy advice, it is important that the advice provided in the pathfinder or learning website is not new to the students. The guidance given should be a reinforcement of what students have been taught in the library and/or classroom. It is also important that teachers and teacher librarians who provide this advice do not assume that all students will read it or even click on the link. Thus there needs to be some practice for students in using the pathfinder or learning website. This is most effective when taught in the

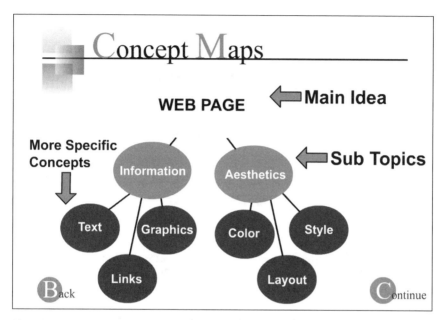

Figure 8.10 Guidance on concept mapping for students at Lincoln High School, USA (http://remc12.k12.mi.us/lhslib/Big%20Six1.htm)

Sections	How to structure a good search engine query:
What is a research project? But where do I start? Working source lists Source Cards Preparing to take notes Plagiarism In-Text Documentation Works Cited lists Working with Online Sources General MLA Style Citation Steps to a Finished Draft Guidelines for Multimedia and Web Page Production Steps in Online Searching Search Strategies Approaching Research	• Brainstorm several key words and phrases, the ones you think would appear in your dream document • Also consider the words that should NOT appear in your dream documents for instance when researching the planet Saturn, you'll want to eliminate references to cars and automobiles. With Dolphins, you'll likely want to avoid football. • Understand syntax, or the language of the search engine. This is revealed in the help or tips page and will guide you to how to use that tool most effectively. • Put most important words and phrases first. • Search nouns first. • Consider phrases which words are likely to appear next to each other in exact order in good results? Names like ?Martin Luther King? ?vitamin A? • Focus on nouns (verbs are often vague, stop words, like articles a, an, the are ignored by most engines) • Consider alternate forms of words (truncate when you can) adolesc' for adolescent, adolescents, adolescence • Check your spelling. Bad spelling usually turns up bad results. • Follow more *like this* leads when you get a good result • Good searchers use advanced search screens. They offer far more power and precision. (Google's Advanced Search) • Use Boolean when you can, especially in databases. Remember that AND is your friend. Use AND to connect words and phrases. • Use field searching (searching titles, for instance) when you can

Figure 8.11 Advice on searching the web from the research guide at Springfield Township High School, USA (www.sdst.org/rguide/searchstrategies.html)

library and then taught again in the classroom, or vice versa. Online learning of this type will be new to many students and the provision of links to searching advice or a table of advice in the learning website itself will not guarantee use. Students can be given search sheets on which they record their topic, the

			Energy Resources				
RESOURCE	HOW DO WE GET IT?	HOW DOES IT GET TO US?	HOW DOES IT PRODUCE ELECTRICITY?	WHAT ARE ITS ADVANTAGES?	WHAT ARE ITS DISADVANTAGES?	IS IT RENEWABLE OR NON-RENEWABLE?	
COAL							
OIL							
GAS							

Figure 8.12 A note-taking grid for students at Forestville Public School, Australia (http://carolynfarrugia.webs.com/worksheet.htm)

keywords or phrases they searched for, where they searched, and brief notes on the websites they found and used. In some schools, students are required to submit these sheets as part of their assignment. Similar sheets can be provided for students to enhance students' note-taking skills. An example of this is shown in Figure 8.12 from Forestville Public School, Australia.

Mediated resources with annotations

As was noted above, pathfinders used to be (and in some cases still are) merely lists of books, websites and other digital resources, which provide the user only with the author and title of books (and perhaps a Dewey number) and title and URL of websites. Although this may be useful information for the most senior students in the school or for university students, it remains a very basic form of information. In schools, if pathfinders are to be part of learning websites, then the resources provided must not only be mediated by the teacher and teacher librarian in relation to the needs and abilities of a student group, but must also provide the students with a guide to the resource's content and advice on how to use it most effectively. The following examples of annotations are taken from the work of this author's teacher librarianship students at Charles Sturt University, Australia, and are reprinted with the students' permission.

When students are given a resource with an annotation, the advice on the content should not merely be a description of it, but it should try to engage the students by making the resource appear relevant in subject matter and to their own study. The first annotation gives information on general content but specifically links part of the book to a student activity. It also states that students 'are made to think':

333.79 JAK

Jakab, C. (2007) Energy use. McMillan, South Yarra, Australia

Essential facts are provided in this well set out resource on how the environment is seriously being threatened and solutions are offered for a sustainable future. Provides information on alternative energy supplies (Activity 4). Questions are raised and you are made to think about the future. Interesting reading and a useful glossary.

In the second annotation, the website has activities for students to complete and this is a differentiated resource, catering for different levels of ability. Identifying and describing resources as suitable for less able students can be difficult, but this annotation used language that will not offend students:

BBC Schools Website School Science Clips Changing Circuits
www.bbc.co.uk/schools/scienceclips/ages/10_11/changing_circuits.shtml

This fun website is to be used with Activity 2. There are three sections in Changing Circuits. 'READ' has simple yet interesting information and also diagrams and symbols used in circuits. You should complete this activity and then progress to 'PLAY' the colourful interactive activity where you must move parts to create different circuits. Finish with 'QUIZ' which can be printed out with your score. Activities are available at different levels to suit a range of abilities.

Advice can also be given to students on using their information literacy skills. Although this is not needed in all annotations, teachers and teacher librarians can make very useful links with information literacy guidance previously given, and can reinforce information literacy skills in annotations. The third annotation provides students with a 'research tip' for evaluating the authority of the website:

Website: **Alternative Energy Sources**. It can be found at:
http://saveenergy.about.com/od/alternativeenergysources/a/altenergysource.htm

In the opening paragraph of this article, Jeffrey Orloff gives some information
about why we need to explore alternative energy sources. Next there is an
explanation of sources of alternatives, which begins with a fairly concise definition
of each one. An adult level of language is used in this site. Research tip: Use your
website evaluation sheet to explore this site. How do you know if this author has
credibility? What could you do to find out? What is About.com? How can you tell if
it is considered to be a reputable source of information?

Annotations can also provide students with a reminder of the information
literacy model that the school might be using, for example Big 6, ISP, PLUS
or DET NSW. The fourth annotation directs students back to the advice given
on the PLUS model in another part of the learning website:

Energy kids (2006) Energy Australia. www.energykids.energyaustralia.com.au/

This site is easily located on the school intranet and ties in with the Electricity and
safety kit, 2002 (363.1ELE). This is a fun interactive site produced by Energy Australia
in 2006 and it includes a comprehensive glossary. Search the site for information on
your project and use the PLUS model questions to keep you on track.

There are no definitive annotations that accompany mediated resources in a
pathfinder or learning website. Teachers and teacher librarians should
experiment with different kinds of annotations and then consult the students
on which style of annotations they prefer. It is likely that in any one list of
annotated resources there will be a mixture of annotations, some mainly
content related, some activity or assignment related, and some which provide
information literacy advice to students. Annotations need to be carefully
worded and should be written in a style and using a level of language that is
suitable for a particular group of students. Annotations that are overly
didactic or patronizing are likely to be ignored by students.

Figure 8.13 Student participation in a wiki at Penrith Public School, Australia (http://penrithpslibrary.pbworks.com/Bushranger-bounties)

Student participation

One of the opportunities offered to teachers and teacher librarians using wikis or websites for their learning websites is to involve students in enhancing the content of the learning website. This enhancement can take the form of comments by students when they use resources listed in a pathfinder or suggestions by students for additions to the resources list as a result of students searching for information on a topic such as renewable energy. In Penrith Public School students were involved in generating newspaper reports on bushrangers, and this project was shared with a neighbouring school. Figure 8.13 shows an example of a student created resource, which was developed using the Newspaper Clipping Generator package (www.fodey.com/generators/newspaper/snippet.asp). The students' work was displayed on the school library wiki and students were able to compare each other's work and discuss their work with the neighbouring school.

A second example of student participation can be seen in Figure 8.14 from Arendal International School, Norway. This year 7 class was exploring the Chinese New Year as part of the curriculum on celebrations. Student participation took the form of a brainstorming exercise in which students used sticky notes to post their ideas on the wiki. This enabled them to see each other's ideas and to have a record of the brainstorming session on the wiki, to which students could return. If this brainstorming session had taken place in the classroom using paper and a blackboard, there would be no record of the students' ideas.

Student participation in learning websites can take many forms and teachers and teacher librarians may wish to consider the value of student participation, which can engage students more in the learning resource and allow them to view themselves as well as their teachers and teacher librarians as creators of resources. Ideas for student participation include:

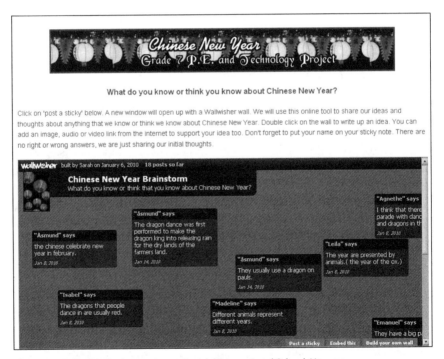

Figure 8.14 Student brainstorming at Arendal International School, Norway
(http://chinesenewyearcelebration.wikispaces.com/What+Do+We+Know%3F)

- brainstorming a topic
- generating research questions for a topic
- posting websites they have found about a topic
- commenting on websites they have used
- commenting on fiction books they have read
- giving examples of student work, for example in art or design.

Conclusion

Developing content for learning websites to be used by students enables teachers and teacher librarians to create locally produced, tailor made resources for their students, thus making a significant contribution to the learning and teaching carried out in the school. The inclusion of pathfinders within learning websites allows staff to mediate resources that students will use, and this in turn makes the learning resource more meaningful to students. Constructivist approaches to learning and teaching encourage student involvement, and learning websites are ideal vehicles for engaging students in using learning resources specifically made to suit their needs, while allowing students to contribute their own comments, ideas and sources. Schools should be encouraged to post these learning websites on the web, in the spirit of sharing resources with other schools across the world, rather than keeping them closed within a school's virtual learning environment or intranet.

References

Methuen High School Media Center (2010) *Pathfinders*,
    www.methuen.k12.ma.us/pathfinders/Alternative%20Energy.htm.
Valenza, J. (2010) *Ten Reasons Why Your Next Pathfinder Should be a Wiki*,
    http://informationfluency.wikispaces.com/Ten+reasons+why+your+next+pathfinder+should+be+a+wiki.

The next phase of ICT in schools

9

Having read this chapter you will be able to:

- reflect on the 21st-century skills needed by students
- evaluate and reflect on future developments such as Web 3.0
- evaluate and reflect on future learning technologies
- focus on the continuing need to develop information literacy in schools
- reflect on the future role of the teacher and teacher librarian.

Introduction

As the previous chapters in this book have shown, there have been rapid developments in ICT in schools and society in general over the past five years. In the 20th century it was possible to look forward perhaps 10 or 20 years and forecast the changes that would occur in technology. In the 21st century this is no longer possible.

Learning and teaching now deal with how we use technology in the school to provide better education for our students, rather than the formats of technology. In attempting to look forward to the next phase of ICT in schools, we must base any discussion about the future of ICT on the learning and teaching context of schools, which was explored in Chapter 2. We cannot say with any certainty what technologies will dominate education in 2031, but can argue that the emphasis on constructivist approaches to education will continue and that students are likely to be more active participants in their learning in 20 years' time. In order to give teachers and teacher librarians some possible views of the future of ICT in schools, this chapter will examine 21st-century skills, future developments of the web, future learning technologies for schools, the future role of teachers and teacher librarians, and the continuing need to develop information literate students.

21st-century skills

There has been much debate about what skills and abilities today's students need in order to be effective learners at school and in higher education, and effective employees in the workplace. The implication is that students need different skills than they did in the 20th century. The key skills identified by the Partnership for 21st Century Skills (2010) are learning and innovation skills, information, media and technology skills, and life and career skills. It can be argued that 20th-century students needed similar skills and that it is mainly in the area of social media that new skills are needed.

Teachers and teacher librarians can usefully reflect on whether the new skills needed, for example to be able to use Facebook or Twitter, are any more demanding than those that students may already have acquired when using the web. McKenzie argues that his 13 skills sum up what 21st-century learners need, including 'inference, invention, innovation, inquiry . . . interpretation . . . insight' (2010). Although this list is rather artificial, consisting of 13 words starting with 'i', McKenzie highlights a number of key skills that students need not just to find information but also to use it effectively. For example 'inference' implies that students can 'know how to read between the lines, put clues together and fathom meanings that are not self-evident. They must look past the words' (McKenzie, 2010). The key point to be made when discussing 21st-century skills is that they should focus on the learning skills needed by students to cope with the ever increasing amount of information, ideas and concepts – in text, graphic and video formats – that they experience in school and society.

Future developments on the web

Ohler (2008) discusses the emergence of Web 3.0 or the semantic web and argues that 'the semantic web makes information more meaningful to people by making it more understandable to machines'. This should enable teachers, teacher librarians and students to be able to find information that is brought together from more diverse sources on the web than at present: 'When it comes to a web search, for example, the semantic web makes a reasonable pass at collating, synthesizing, and cross-referencing the results for you' (Ohler, 2008).

Web 3.0 therefore promises to improve vastly the current web tools. Future search engines may be able to synthesize information and ideas from a range of sources. Instead of listing websites, search engines may be able to send users a synthesized report, which compares and contrasts different ideas and information. Although some Web 3.0 tools are available, they have to date had little impact on education, and many of the promised improvements in web searching have yet to appear. Some search engines have adopted a visual format, but most are mainly still static. None of them can carry out an interactive reference interview with a student so they are a long way from being teacher librarians. Schools may have to wait until Web 5 or Web 6 to see the emergence of intelligent tools, which can ask questions in order to understand the searcher's purpose.

Other developments on the web are suggested by Chapman (2009), including viewing the web on a much larger screen and looking at websites by scrolling horizontally instead of vertically. There may also be many more interactive magazines on the web, which unlike their printed equivalents will incorporate graphics linked to other sources such as video. Chapman suggests that these magazines may each host their own social media.

More online collaboration is likely to take place on the web, using tools such as Wridea (http://wridea.com), which allows real-time brainstorming and could be used for collaborative projects involving schools from different areas or countries. The trend of watching television programmes on the web will continue apace with programmes produced directly for viewing on the web, and only available on the web. Although they may be mainly entertainment programmes, the opportunity to make 'TV' web programmes for educational purposes will be possible, and with new tools is likely to be much easier than today.

Chapman also suggests that the web will become the main source of information for most people in the world, stating, 'Newspapers and magazines will likely be the first media replaced by the Web. Not far behind will be TV and movies.' Books, however, are likely to continue to be popular in print.

In the next few years school staff will need to keep up to date with these changes in the way the web can be used, and teacher librarians will have a key role to play in keeping them informed of new developments.

Future learning technologies in schools

Ley (2010, 133) provides a wide ranging overview of the technologies and trends that will affect education over the next ten years. The key technological development he envisages is in mobile computing, and he argues that soon learning technology will include 'mobile phones, smart phones, ultra-mobile PCs and mobile internet devices, handheld games consoles, internet tablets, media players, e-book readers and digital cameras'. The trend to integrate different technologies within one device, as in smart phones, will continue. The likely technological improvements in devices include more touch screen applications, greater availability of handwriting and voice recognition, and a leap in the quality of screen images, for example high definition photos and videos as an integral part of most devices.

The challenges to be faced by schools include making their technology as up to date as it is in society. For example, if mobile learning is to become reality, then school virtual learning environments (VLEs) will have to enable students to connect to the VLE and not just with a web link. Students will expect to be able to access all their stored work, all resources designed by teachers and teacher librarians, the school's virtual library, and online classroom sessions in their own and other schools.

For many schools, the current issues of funding will be paramount, as will technical expertise and staffing. Whether tomorrow's schools will have equal access to technologies such as cloud computing is debatable. LeBlanc (2008) has an optimistic vision of future schools, in which,

> Arriving at class . . . students will enter a classroom that is no longer setup lecture style, but forum based and focused towards a holographic projector that will enable discussions to be had by members of academic communities that reside in other countries, as easily as if they were in the same room. With this technology, it's possible to have the best professors in the world teaching at schools around the world simultaneously.

Equality of access to technologies between and within countries is likely to be relevant for the foreseeable future.

Future roles for the teacher and teacher librarian

Although there have been building programmes for future schools in North America, Australia and the UK, they have focused on the physical environment in the school, including how to provide an effective ICT infrastructure. There has been less focus on what the future roles of teachers and teacher librarians might be. Such (2010) outlines a range of issues that will face teachers in the schools of the future, including the changing nature of schools, as schools will no longer be seen as the only place where students learn; the changing role of secondary school teachers, who may increasingly have to adopt roles outside their subject expertise; and changes in technology: 'Adapting to utilise the tools and technologies used outside of classrooms – in homes, workplaces and social spaces – will become increasingly important' (2010, 4). Teachers in the future will retain their subject knowledge but are likely to use external experts more to support their teaching, and are likely to engage students more in the search for greater subject knowledge, so in the future more teachers will learn alongside their students.

It is not clear what changes there will be to the physical nature of information in the future. Today's school libraries still retain a sizeable stock of printed books, and managing this collection is often viewed as the key role of the teacher librarian. There are various predictions about when or if printed books will no longer be used, but the majority view is that this is unlikely to happen within the next ten years. However, there will definitely be a reduction in the number of printed books in future school libraries and it is likely that some schools will be further ahead than others in becoming virtual libraries. It is obvious that there will still be a school library collection for teacher librarians to manage, to provide students and staff with access to the learning resources they need. Teacher librarians will be required to manage systems that make these resources available. They may face a challenge in convincing school managers of the importance of their role to the school, whether or not there are printed books in the library. Hay and Foley (2009) argue that future teacher librarians will face an environment in which e-books become more common, it will be necessary for integrated systems to be introduced in schools that provide students with a single access to learning resources, and schools will need to incorporate information ethics into the school curriculum.

Collaboration between teachers and teacher librarians will be even more important in the future. The increased use of learning resources within schools, including the joint creation of resources by teachers and teacher librarians, and a gradual increase in e-learning and mobile learning in secondary or high schools, will lead to more interdependence between teachers and teacher librarians.

Developing information literate students

It is difficult to predict what the future developments in ICT will be, but future students will certainly be faced with even more information, within and outside the school, than they have at present, and will require the skills and abilities to cope with what may appear to be an overwhelming choice of information sources. It will be important for students to be continually developing as information literate members of the school community and wider society, so teachers and teacher librarians will need to continue to educate students to be effective searchers for information. As noted above, in the school library of the future, students will find information through an integrated platform giving them access to resources that are online on the free web, or in secure stores with password access.

Students will continue to be required to be effective planners, evaluators, interpreters and synthesizers as expectations rise about their involvement in their learning. Teachers and teacher librarians will engage future students more in discussions about accessing and interpreting learning resources and information sources, so they might be more reflective in their use of sources. This is a difficult challenge for teachers and teacher librarians, as many people think that information is ubiquitous and easily sourced and understood; this view is likely to be reinforced by the educational use of ICT devices such as smart phones (which future students may well refer to as an i-set or i-tool). The terms used in future are more likely to be defined by marketing specialists than teachers or teacher librarians. Information literacy, which this author views as incorporating other literacies such as digital, media or visual literacy, will become more of a focus when schools determine their curriculum, and how they can best manage learning and teaching, in the schools of the future.

Conclusion

The next phase of ICT in schools will provide teachers and teacher librarians with new tools to access information resources and create learning resources in schools. Although schools may look physically different in the future, the fundamental aims of schools, which include the development of students as effective and reflective learners, will remain.

References

Chapman, C. (2009) *The Future of The Web: where will we be in five years?*, www.noupe.com/trends/the-future-of-the-web-where-will-we-be-in-five-years.html.

Hay, L. and Foley, C. (2009) School Libraries Building Capacity for Student Learning in 21C, *Scan*, **28**(2), 17–24.

LeBlanc, M. (2008) *The Future of Technology and Education*, www.neowin.net/news/the-future-of-technology-and-education.

Ley, D. (2010) Emerging Technologies for Learning. In Parkes, D. and Walton, W. (eds) *Web 2.0 and Libraries: impacts, technologies and trends*, Chandos Publishing.

McKenzie, J. (2010) The 21st Century Bookmark, *From Now On*, **19** (3), http://fno.org/Jan2010/bookmark.html.

Ohler, J. (2008) The Semantic Web in Education, *Educause Quarterly*, **31** (4), www.educause.edu/EDUCAUSE+Quarterly/ EDUCAUSEQuarterlyMagazineVolum/TheSemanticWebinEducation/163437.

Partnership for 21st Century Skills (2010) *Framework for 21st Century Learning*, www.p21.org/index.php?option=com_content&task=view&id=254&Itemid=119.

Such, D. (2010) *Education Futures, Teachers and Technology*, www.futurelab.org.uk/resources/documents/other_research_reports/Education _futures.pdf.

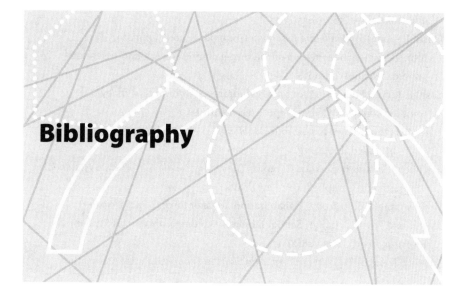

Bibliography

Bilal, D., Sarangthem, S. and Bachir, I. (2008) Toward a Model of Children's Information Seeking Behavior in Using Digital libraries. In *Proceedings of the Second International Symposium on Information Interaction in Context*, ACM, 145–51.

Boswell, W. (2010) How to Search the Web Faster, Easier, and More Efficiently, http://websearch.about.com/od/searchingtheweb/tp/web_search_simple.htm.

Brisco, S. (2007) Which Wiki Is Right For You?, *School Library Journal*, www.schoollibraryjournal.com/article/CA6438167.html.

Brown, J. (2002) *Why Evaluate Web Information*, www.ed.uiuc.edu/wp/credibility/page2.html.

Butt, G. (2006) *Lesson Planning*, 2nd edn, Continuum International.

Capel, S., Leask, M. and Turner, T. *Learning to Teach in the Secondary School: a companion to school experience*, Routledge.

Carlson, C. (2002) Notes from the Trenches: the seven commandments of highly effective searching, www.llrx.com/columns/notes54.htm.

Chapman, C. (2009) *The Future of The Web: where will we be in five years?*, www.noupe.com/trends/the-future-of-the-web-where-will-we-be-in-five-years.html.

Chung, J. and Neuman, D. (2007) High School Students' Information Seeking and Use for Class Projects, *Journal of the American Society for Information Science and Technology*, 58 (10), 1503–17.

Durst, J. (2009) *Penleigh and Essendon Grammar School: animoto*,
      http://slav.globalteacher.org.au/picture-gallery/penleigh-and-essendon-
      grammar-school-animoto.

Eash, E. (2006) Podcasting 101 for K-12 Librarians, *Information Today*,
      www.infotoday.com/cilmag/apr06/eash.shtml.

Edublogs (2008) *Ways to Use Your Edublogs*,
            http://edublogs.org.

Eisenberg, M. and Berkowitz, B. (2010) *The Definitive Big 6 Workshop Handbook*,
      4th edn Campbell, CA: Paw Prints.

Gibson-Langford, L. (2007) Collaboration: force or forced? Part 2, *Scan*, **27** (1), 31–7.

Hay, L. and Foley, C. (2009) School Libraries Building Capacity for Student
      Learning in 21C, *Scan*, **28**(2), 17–24.

Herring, J. (1996) *Teaching Information Skills in Schools*, Library Association
      Publishing.

Herring, J. (2004) *The Internet and Information Skills: a guide for teachers and
      school librarians*. Facet Publishing.

Herring, J. (2010a) Year 12 Students' Use of Information Literacy Skills: a
      constructivist grounded analysis. In Lloyd, A. and Talja, S. (eds) *Practising
      Information Literacy: bringing theories of learning, practice and information
      literacy together*, Centre for Information Studies, Charles Sturt University.

Herring, J. (2010b) School Students, Question Formulation and Issues of Transfer: a
      constructivist grounded analysis, *Libri*, in press.

Herring, J. and Bush, S. (2009) Creating a Culture of Transfer for Information
      Literacy Skills in Schools. In Ainsworth, A., Crothers, G., Lopez, C., Pritchard, M.
      and Scott, C. (eds) *Engage explore celebrate: ASLA XXI Biennial Conference
      Proceedings 2009*.

Herring, J. and Tarter, A. (2007) Progress in Developing Information Literacy in a
      Secondary School Using the PLUS Model, *School Libraries in View*, **23**, 23–7.

Hill, P. (2010) *Thoughts on Using Prezi as a Teaching Tool*,
      http://prezi.com/rfsnedhqmhqa/thoughts-on-using-prezi-as-a-teaching-tool.

Hock, R. (2007) *The Extreme Searcher's Internet Handbook: a guide for the serious
      searcher*, 2nd edn, Cyberage Books.

Holmes, A. and Tobin, E. (2005) Motivation Through Collaboration at St George's
      School of Montreal, *School Libraries in Canada*, **25** (2),
      www.clatoolbox.ca/casl/slic/SLICVol25issue2.pdf.

James. M. (2007) *Improving Learning How to Learn: classrooms, schools and networks*, Routledge.

Johnson, D. and Lamb, A. (2007) *Evaluating Internet Resources*, http://eduscapes.com/tap/topic32.htm.

Killen, R. (2007) *Effective Teaching Strategies: lessons from research and practice*, 4th edn, Thomson Social Science Press.

Kuhlthau, C. (2004) *Seeking Meaning: a process approach to library and information services*, 2nd edn, Libraries Unlimited.

Kuhlthau,K., Maniotes, L. and Caspari, A. (2007) *Guided inquiry: learning in the 21st century*, Libraries Unlimited.

Kuiper, E., Volman, M. and Terwel, J. (2008) Students' Use of Web Literacy Skills and Strategies: searching, reading and evaluating Web information, *Information Research*, **13** (3), http://informationr.net/ir/13-3/paper351.html.

Lamb, A. and Johnson, B. (2007) *An Information Skills Workout: wikis and collaborative writing*, http://eduscapes.com/hightech/spaces/collaborative/wikiTL.pdf.

Langford, L. (1998) Information Literacy: a clarification. *School Libraries Worldwide*, **4** (1), 59–72.

LeBlanc, M. (2008) *The Futureof Technology and Education*, www.neowin.net/news/the-future-of-technology-and-education.

Ley, D. (2010) Emerging Technologies for Learning. In Parkes, D. and Walton, W. (eds) *Web 2.0 and Libraries: impacts, technologies and trends*, Chandos Publishing.

Lowe, K., Lee, L., Schibeci, R., Cummings, R., Phillips, R. and Lake, D. (2010) Learning Objects and Engagement of Students in Australian and New Zealand Schools, *British Journal of Educational Technology*, **41** (2), 227–41.

Lynch, P. and Horton, S. (2008) *Web Style Guide: basic design principles for designing websites*, 3rd edn, Yale University Press, www.webstyleguide.com/wsg3/index.html.

Marcinek, A. (2009) *Hello Animoto*, Classroom 2.0, www.classroom20.com/forum/topics/hello-animoto.

Markless, S. (ed.) (2009) *The Innovative School Librarian*, Facet Publishing.

McKenzie, J. (2010) The 21st Century Bookmark, *From Now On*, **19** (3), http://fno.org/Jan2010/bookmark.html.

McPherson, K. (2006) Wikis and Literacy Development, *Teacher Librarian*, **34** (2), 70–2.

Methuen High School Media Center (2010) *Pathfinders*,

www.methuen.k12.ma.us/pathfinders/Alternative%20Energy.htm.

Montiel-Overall, P. (2008) A Qualitative Study of Teacher and Librarian Collaboration, *Scan*, **27** (3), 25–31.

New South Wales, Department of Education and Training (2006) *About Quality Teaching*,
https://www.det.nsw.edu.au/proflearn/areas/qt/qt.htm.

New South Wales, Department of Education and Training (2007a) *Information Skills in the School*,
www.curriculumsupport.education.nsw.gov.au/schoollibraries/teachingideas/isp/index.htm.

New South Wales, Department of Education and Training (2007b) *Information Skills in the School*,
www.curriculumsupport.education.nsw.gov.au/schoollibraries/teachingideas/info_skills/assets/infoprocesscycle.pdf.

Notess, G. (2006) *Teaching Web Search Skills*, Information Today, Inc.

Novak, J. and Canas, A. (2008) *The Theory Underlying Concept Maps and How to Construct and Use Them*, Institute for Human and Machine Cognition.

O'Connell, J. (2006) Engaging the Google Generation Through Web 2.0, *Scan*, **25** (3), 46–50.

Ohler, J. (2008) The Semantic Web in Education, *Educause Quarterly*, **31** (4),
www.educause.edu/EDUCAUSE+Quarterly/EDUCAUSEQuarterlyMagazineVolum/TheSemanticWebinEducation/163437.

Pappas, P. (2000) *Design Your Website From the Bottom Up*,
www.edteck.com/eddesign/web_docs/Bottom_up.pdf.

Partnership for 21st Century Skills (2010) *Framework for 21st Century Learning*,
www.p21.org/index.php?option=com_content&task=view&id=254&Itemid=119.

Porter, J. (2003) *Testing the Three Click Rule*,
www.uie.com/articles/three_click_rule.

Prensky, M. (2009) H. Sapiens Digital: from digital immigrants and digital natives to digital wisdom, *Innovate*, **5** (3),
www.innovateonline.info/index.php?view=article&id=705.

Pritchard, A. (2009) *Ways of Learning: learning theories and learning styles in the classroom*, 2nd edn, Routledge.

Robinson, A. (2010) *Effective Research: advanced search*,
http://library-online.org.uk/2010/06/welcome-to-sixth-form-historians.

Rockingham County Public Schools (2010) *Using Animoto in RCPS*,
www.rockingham.k12.va.us/screencasts/animoto/animoto.htm.

Ryan, K. and Cooper, J. (2010) *Those Who Can, Teach*, Wadsworth Cengage Learning.

Schmidt, R., Kowlaski, V. and Nevins, L. (2010) Guiding the Inquiry Using the Modified SLR, *School Libraries Worldwide*, **16** (1), 13–32.

Schrock, K. (2009a) *Critical Evaluation Surveys*, http://school.discoveryeducation.com/schrockguide/eval.html.

Schrock, K. (2009b) *The 5 Ws of Website Evaluation*, http://kathyschrock.net/abceval/5ws.pdf.

Scottish Library and Information Council (2006) *Validity of Information*, www.ictl.org.uk/U1O3CG/page_02.htm.

Shambles.net (2010) *Google Earth Lessons*, www.shambles.net/pages/learning/GeogP/gearthplan.

Smith, W. (2006) *How to Storyboard Your Website*, http://e-articles.info/e/a/title/How-to-Storyboard-Your-Web-Site.

Spence, C. (2009) *Leading with Passion and Purpose*, Pembroke.

Steffens, P. (2008) *Diigo – 21st Century Tool for Research, Reading and Collaboration*, www.amphi.com/~technology/techtalks/online/nov08/bestpract.htm.

Such, D. (2010) *Education Futures, Teachers and Technology*, www.futurelab.org.uk/resources/documents/other_research_reports/Education _futures.pdf.

TeachersFirst (2010), www.teachersfirst.com/content/wiki/wikiideas1.cfm.

UC Berkeley Library (2009) Finding Information on the Internet: a tutorial, www.lib.berkeley.edu/TeachingLib/Guides/Internet/Strategies.html.

University of Queensland Library (2008) *Internet Resource Evaluation: how-to guide*, www.library.uq.edu.au/ssah/useits/inteval.pdf.

Valenza, J. (2010) *Ten Reasons Why Your Next Pathfinder Should be a Wiki*, http://informationfluency.wikispaces.com/Ten+reasons+why+your+next+pathfi nder+should+be+a+wiki.

Web2 Tutorial (2008) *Web 2.0 Tutorial*, http://web2tutorial.wikispaces.com.

Wetzel, D. (2005) *How to Weave the Web into K-8 Science*, NSTA Press.

Index